Contents

GW01376193

Introduction

Nelson Living Geography is a brand new series for Key Stage 3. It comprises a student textbook and a homework and assessment book for each year of the key stage. There is also a web site to provide updated information relevant to the series.

The three textbooks which make up the series have been carefully written and designed to provide clear **progression** as students move on through the key stage. This has been achieved partly through the selection of National Curriculum content for each book, and partly through the depth to which this content is examined. Consideration has been given to language levels used, and vocabulary and sentence structure develop in complexity between *Book 1* and *Book 3*. The use of slightly smaller type in succeeding books allows each page in *Book 2* to contain more text than in *Book 1*, and a page in *Book 3* to contain more than in *Book 2*. Thus subject matter is dealt with in more detail as the student progresses from Year 7 to Year 9.

Differentiation is also achieved within each textbook through the questions. The tasks set at the end of each spread are designed to be answered across a range of levels, with short, simple answers possible, as well as giving the most able students the opportunity to write more detailed responses. This *Homework and Assessment Book* for the teacher contains a 'Commentary on the Questions' section for each unit, which discusses the different levels of response that might be expected to questions in the textbook and on the homework sheets. In addition, there is a page of questions headed 'Extensions' at the end of each unit in the textbooks. These questions are aimed at those students who look for a greater challenge, and either they require a deeper understanding of the skill or concept involved, or they take a more synoptic approach and require links to be made between two or more of the spreads.

Within *Book 2* the student is building on the knowledge and skills base of *Book 1*. The basic mapwork skills are included in many of the units so that information about landscapes can be unravelled. Map reading becomes one of the geographer's tools and not an end in itself. More concepts are introduced throughout the book but rather than understand these ideas on their own, students are asked to apply them to management situations. Environmental issues are dealt with separately within Unit 5 but are also covered as integral parts of other units. The whole idea of people managing the

environments around them pervades the book and students are encouraged to identify the ways in which people manage landscapes at all levels. They look at small scale local management, regional, national and global systems. They begin to see the links between cause and effect and between issues at different scales. Students are encouraged to think about the implications of the behaviour of people and its link to physical and human landscapes, plus the link between physical and human landscapes and people. Students will be thinking as they learn throughout *Book 2*. They will begin to question development. They will begin to unravel the concept of sustainability and they will be introduced to the complexity of managing environments. They will understand the role of political, social, environmental and economic influences on decision making. Finally, as global citizens, they will be able to consider their own actions and ways in which they as individuals can make an impact on the planet.

This series does not offer a package just to be taught, but is very much designed with the active participation of the student in mind. Each unit starts with a carefully selected image or montage of images that is designed to stimulate discussion in class. The 'Commentary on the Questions' pages give some background to the pictures, and suggest opportunities offered by them. Ideas that may be introduced into the discussion by the teacher are also suggested.

Key features of the organisation of each spread are the **Focus** and **Summary** boxes. At a simple level, the focus box is an introduction that sets the scene for the spread. More importantly, each focus box raises between two and four key questions that are to be addressed in the spread, and helps to promote an enquiry approach to learning. Most important of all, the summary box then returns to each question raised in the focus, and provides short, snappy answers. The detail and the discussion are in the body of the text, the photographs and diagrams, and in the responses drawn out by the questions, while focus and summary boxes link them together. They make an instant 'soundbite' which can aid understanding of the concepts raised in the spread, and also act as a quick revision tool.

A further key feature is the **Find out more** toolbar. This provides important cross-references that have been built into the book. It enables teachers to use the book in a more flexible way, because it may often be more appropriate to follow these cross-references

Focus

- How does a river alter the shape of the land it flows through?
- What happens if the river has to flow over some very hard rock?
- What other processes are shaping the river landscape?

Summary

- Rivers cut valleys into the landscape
- Waterfalls are formed where a river crosses some resistant rock
- Weathering by plants, acids and temperature changes also shape the river landscape.

than simply to go on to the next page. It also helps students find their way around the book and develop an awareness and appreciation of the links that are so important in geography. This toolbar allows students to look ahead and see how new areas of study relate to their current area of study; it also allows them to look back and see how a previously studied topic has a bearing on the fuller understanding of the topic currently under consideration. Some new topics can therefore be introduced in a context that is already familiar.

Throughout the book, key words are highlighted when they first appear. This highlighting indicates to students that there is an explanation of that key word available in the **Glossary** at the end of each unit.

There is also a Website to accompany the series. This website allows teachers and students to have easy access to further information on the topics covered in the series. There are updates to existing material in the books, and new case studies are provided on a regular basis. It also provides reviews and hotlinks to other useful geography sites on the internet. Go to: www.livinggeography.co.uk

Assessment

The full course contains nine Assessments, three in each book. Between them they cover a range of human, physical and environmental topics, and they are in a variety of styles. They build up to make a significant contribution towards the evidence needed to assign students to a particular level.

The Assessments are not designed to be supervised tests, but will probably need a minimum of two weeks of lesson and homework time. They have been designed to be carried out independently, but students will benefit from time spent in class discussing the tasks and having the expectations clarified. The actual level of support offered to students is entirely at the discretion of the individual department, since the results will have currency and need to be comparable only within the school. As far as possible, the level of support needed or offered should be taken into account when assigning the work to a level.

The Assessments give students the opportunity to show their skills, as detailed in paragraphs 1 (a) to (f) and 2 (a) to (g) of the Key Stage 3 Programme of Study, to show their understanding of the topics covered, and to show their ability to apply that understanding. The nature of these Assessments means that it is harder for them to generate evidence of a student's knowledge, and it may be that the traditional end of term test or end of year exam shows this better. The Homework and Assessment Books have detailed guidance on marking the Assessments and show how different responses can be matched to different levels in the National Curriculum. The guidance in *Book 1* concentrates on levels 2 to 5, in *Book 2* it concentrates on levels 3 to 6, and in *Book 3* it concentrates on levels 4 to 7. In practice students can respond to the tasks at levels outside these ranges, and a correct level can be determined by relating their work to the level descriptions published in the National Curriculum.

The Assessments in *Book 2* arise out of the units on Coasts, Shops and Services, and Environmental Issues. The Coastal Assessment explores the link between the physical and human environment along a stretch of coast. It asks students to take the role of a local planning officer replying to a concerned local resident. It uses a variety of data from a collection of secondary resources: landuse map, geology map, photographs and written documents. All resources necessary to complete this Assessment are included in the textbook. The second Assessment, arising out of the Shops and Services unit, links the theme of a coastal settlement with retailing and industrial issues. It is a planning simulation taking the form of a decision making exercise. It is presented graphically with annotated explanations and can be developed using oral assessment methods. Students are given secondary resources including a map extract and photos plus some statistics. From these they are asked to design a new marina and associated developments in the small harbour town of Watchet. The third Assessment, at the end of the Environmental Issues unit, takes the case study of the globally important environment of Antarctica and asks the student to consider how it could be developed for tourism. Students are asked to produce a radio broadcast, stimulated by the secondary resources contained in the textbook. They are also encouraged to use the Internet to find out further up-to-date information about tourism on this continent. The Assessment is suitable for group work and oral assessment.

Spread across the three years of Key Stage 3, the Assessments in the three books will generate much of the evidence needed to make a judgement on the level achieved by a student. By completing the Assessments at fairly regular intervals, the teacher can keep a running check on the progress made by students as they move through the key stage, as well as making the end of key stage judgement. The Assessments will not be the only evidence available, and it is important also to consider the further evidence available from the responses to the questions which come at the end of each spread and in the Extensions at the end of each unit. These offer the student extra opportunities to show the skills and understanding required to satisfy particular level descriptions.

Photocopiable worksheets

The worksheets in the *Homework and Assessment Book* extend the ideas introduced in the *Student Book*. Many students will be able to complete these independently, applying the knowledge, understanding and skills developed in the corresponding spread(s) in the textbook. However, the worksheets do take the ideas further, and it may often be appropriate to discuss them before the students complete them. Many of the worksheets allow answers at different levels, and differentiation is therefore by outcome.

Commentary on questions

The answer given is not usually written in the language of the Year 8 student, and is often not the answer that a student would offer if left to answer the question alone. The Commentary suggests ideas that could be teased out of students in a class discussion, or teaching points that arise from the questions. The questions have been designed to be more than mere 'exercises to do'; many will work much better if they are built into lessons as discussion, teaching and learning activities. Once ideas have been aired in discussion, students will be in a much better position to write a good answer. An exercise book with more detailed and 'correct' responses achieved that way is more useful than a

book with half-developed, hesitant and sometimes plain 'wrong' ideas written by the student working on their own.

ICT

The revised National Curriculum (DfEE/QCA 1999) increased the emphasis on students' development of ICT skills. The Key Stage 3 Programme of Study for Geography highlights places where ICT could be used, including:
- selecting and using secondary sources of evidence
- drawing maps and plans and selecting and using graphical techniques to present evidence on maps and diagrams
- communicating in different ways
- developing decision-making skills

There are numerous opportunities throughout *Book 2* for developing such skills and teachers will be able to choose appropriate activities to develop ICT skills. The Assessments particularly lend themselves to this approach, although many other activities could also be addressed using ICT – for example; the calculation for 2a on page 9 could be completed using a spreadsheet.

The letter on page 17, question 4b, could be word processed. The multiplier effect diagram in 4c could be drawn using a drawing program. The assessment for question 3 on page 18 could be word processed; maps could be drawn, images scanned, photographs taken with digital cameras and imported. Question 3 in page 27 could be completed using a table constructed from a word processing package.

Question 2 on page 33 could be completed using IT. Photographs from the book could be scanned and used to help produce this. The pie charts for question 1, page 41, could be completed using Excel or a similar program. The questionnaire and its matrix can be word processed. The results from the matrix could then be put into a spreadsheet. Page 47, question 2 could re recorded in a simple spreadsheet.

The leaflet on page 63 could be word processed and could contain images and maps imported from the internet or CD Roms.

The building for question 4, page 79, could be drawn using an IT package, as could the logo for 5a on page 81.

See also the guidance on developing Information Technology as a Key Skill on page 8.

National Curriculum coverage

Between them, *Nelson Living Geography Books 1* to *3* cover all requirements of the Key Stage 3 Programme of Study of the revised National Curriculum (DfEE/QCA 1999). The grid below shows the coverage provided by the series, with the contribution made by *Book 2* shown in more detail. *Book 3* covers some new material (tectonics and population) but much of the book is made up of studies of two countries in different states of development, South Africa and the USA. This satisfies statements 3 and 6a of the Key Stage 3 Programme of Study, but also enables much of the physical, human and environmental geography covered in *Books 1* and *2* to be re-visited in a new context.

Programme of study reference	Book 1	Book 2	Book 3
	Key: ✓ = covered in book	*Key:* numbers = pages, or ◄———► = throughout	*Key:* ✓ = covered in book
1. Undertaking geographical enquiry			
(a) *Ask geographical questions and identify issues*	✓	38–39, 44–45, 47, 86–89	✓
(b) *Suggest appropriate sequences of investigation*	✓	44–45, 47, 86–89	✓
(c) *Collect, record and present evidence*	✓		✓
(d) *Analyse and evaluate evidence, draw and justify conclusions*	✓		✓
(e) *Appreciate effects of values and attitudes, clarify and develop own values and attitudes*	✓	38–39, 41, 44–45 47, 56–57, 75, 86–89	✓
(f) *Communicate in appropriate ways*	✓		✓
2. Developing geographical skills			
(a) *Use an extended geographical vocabulary*	✓	◄———►	✓
(b) *Select and use appropriate fieldwork techniques and instruments*	✓	44–45, 47, 75, 86–89	
(c) *Use atlas, globes, maps and plans...*	✓	◄———►	✓
(d) *Select and use secondary sources of evidence...*	✓	38–39, 56–57, 92–93	✓
(e) *Draw maps and plans at a range of scales...*	✓	18, 23, 38–39, 45, 56–57, 69, 86–89, 97	✓
(f) *Communicate in different ways, including using ICT*	✓	◄———►	✓
(g) *Decision-making, including using ICT*	✓	48, 56–57, 76, 86–89 108–109	✓
3. Knowledge and understanding of places			
(a) *The location of places and environments*	✓	◄———►	✓
(b) *The national, international and global contexts of places studied*	✓	6, 8, 10, 12, 14 16, 58–73, 94–110	✓
(c) *The physical and human features giving rise to the distinctive character of places*	✓	◄———►	✓
(d) *How and why changes happen, and the issues arising*	✓	◄———►	✓
(e) *Explain how places are interdependent...*	✓	◄———►	✓
4. Knowledge and understanding of patterns and processes			
(a) *Describe and explain patterns of physical and human features*	✓	◄———►	✓
(b) *Identify, describe and explain physical and human*	✓	◄———►	✓

Programme of study reference	Book 1	Book 2	Book 3
5. Environmental change and sustainable development			
(a) Describe and explain environmental change and recognise different ways of managing it	✓	10, 16, 20–34, 37–38, 42, 56–70, 74–92, 108	✓
(b) Explore the idea of sustainable development and recognise its implications	✓	10, 12, 32, 64, 68, 76, 78, 80, 84, 86–89 92, 108	✓
6. (a) Countries			
Two countries in significantly different states of economic development			✓
6. (b) Tectonic processes			
i Global distribution of tectonic activity			✓
ii The nature, causes and effects of earthquakes or volcanic eruptions			✓
iii Human responses to the associated hazards			✓
6. (c) Geomorphological processes			
i Processes responsible for the development of selected landforms...	✓	20–26	
ii The causes and effects of a hazard, and human responses to it	✓	28–38	✓
6. (d) Weather and climate			
i The differences between weather and climate	✓		
ii The components and links in the water cycle	✓		
iii How and why aspects of weather and climate vary from place to place	✓		✓
6. (e) Ecosystems			
i The characteristics and distribution of one major biome		60, 66, 70	✓
ii How the ecosystems of this biome are related to climate, soil and human activity		62, 64, 68, 70	✓
6. (f) Population			
i The global distribution of population		94–96	✓
ii The causes and effects of changes in the population of regions and countries...		98–108	✓
iii The interrelationship between people und resources		108	✓
6. (g) Settlement			
i Reasons for the location, growth and nature of individual settlements	✓	52	✓
ii The provision of goods and services		40–50	
iii Changes in the functions of settlements...	✓	50–52	✓
iv Patterns and changes in urban land use	✓		✓
6. (h) Economic activities			
i Types and classifications of economic activity		4	✓
ii The geographical distribution of one or more economic activities	✓	6–16	✓
iii How and why the distribution has changed and is changing	✓	8, 12, 14, 74–84, 92, 93	✓

Programme of study reference	Book 1	Book 2	Book 3
6. (i) Development			
i Ways of identifying differences within and between countries			✓
ii The effect of differences in development on quality of life...		98–104, 108	✓
iii Factors that influence development		98–104	✓
6. (j) Environmental issues			
i How conflicting demands on an environment arise	✓	10, 30–32, 38–39, 56–57, 62, 64, 68, 70, 74–92, 108	✓
ii How and why attempts are made to plan and manage environments			✓
iii The effects of environmental planning and management			✓
6. (k) Resource issues			
i The sources and supply of a resource	✓	60, 62, 64, 66, 70	✓
ii Effects on the environment of the use of a resource	✓	62, 64, 68, 70, 92	✓
iii Resource planning and management	✓	64, 68, 70, 92	✓

Statement 7 in the Programme of Study lists four requirements that should be met across the whole key stage:

a. Study at a range of scales;

b. Study of different parts of the world and different types of environment;

c. Carry out fieldwork investigations outside the classroom;

d. Study issues of topical significance.

Nelson Living Geography has been designed so that the first two requirements are met both within individual books and across the series. Opportunities are suggested for fieldwork investigations, and case studies have been chosen to reflect topical issues. The dedicated *Living Geography* website (www.livinggeography.co.uk) enables these issues to be updated, and further topical issues to be introduced.

Key Skills and Geography at Key Stage 3

At all levels, geography is a natural vehicle for the delivery of key skills. *Nelson Living Geography* offers many opportunities for students to develop the six key skills, and the signposts for *Book 2* below suggest some of the ways that they may be incorporated into a teaching programme. Signposting is at National Framework Level 1, which equates broadly to the standard of Foundation tier at GCSE. Level 2 would relate to the standard of Higher tier GCSE, while Level 3 relates to AS and A levels. These National Framework levels are therefore different from the National Curriculum levels, but there is a broad equivalence between National Framework and Key Skills Level 1, and National Curriculum Levels 3 to 6.

There are three core key skills: Application of Number, Information Technology, and Communication; and three wider key skills: Working with Others, Improving Own Learning and Performance, and Problem Solving. Incorporating key skills development into a teaching programme has a number of potential advantages:

- The earlier the students are encouraged to develop these skills, the better prepared they are for when these skills are formally assessed.
- Thinking of ways of incorporating key skills can stimulate new approaches to teaching, learning and assessment.
- Developing key skills usually requires a greater degree of participation and commitment on the part of the students. This can lead to a more active learning process which the students find enjoyable, and this in turn can encourage more students to continue studying geography throughout their school careers.

The specification for each of the key skills is divided into three parts:
- Part A: *What you need to know* – lists what students need to learn and practise.
- Part B: *What you must do* – describes the skills they must show for assessment.
- Part C: *Guidance* – describes some of the activities and evidence that might be suitable.

The page numbers below refer to the student textbook and to this homework and assessment book. Homework book references are in *italic*. The suggestions are not exhaustive, and many other opportunities may be found. To a large extent, these opportunities will depend on how a teacher chooses to work with a class. In 'Communication', for example, there is a requirement for discussion; some teachers will build this naturally into almost every lesson, while others will prefer it to be an occasional, more formal occurrence. Similarly, the requirements

of 'Information Technology' will be more regularly met in those schools where access to computers is easier, and by teachers who feel comfortable with the technology.

There will be many opportunities when evidence for several of the key skills can be collected at the same time. For example, if students carried out the fieldwork to measure the state of the environment (pages 86–89) in groups, evidence may be generated quite naturally for Application of Number, Information Technology, Communication and Working with Others. It is also possible to incorporate aspects of Improving Own Learning and Performance and Problem Solving.

Application of Number (N)

Coverage of Part A is almost complete; students will use diagrams like graphs, charts and maps in many of the spreads, and numbers in their different forms occur regularly, for example as grid references, scales, temperatures and velocities. Students will be asked to make accurate observations and to carry out calculations using data provided, such as finding the mean of environmental and factual assessments, and working out the angles for pie charts.

Information Technology (IT)

The specification requires that students find out information from different sources (not only IT sources) and choose that which is relevant for their purpose. They must then manipulate the information and present it appropriately. While there is no requirement to use IT in any part of the textbook, and all activities can be carried out without it, there are several places where the use of IT is suggested. Other opportunities to use IT will be found by the teachers who wish to emphasise this approach to learning. Some of the work that may be carried out using IT, for example word processing or desk-top publishing, does not come directly into the requirements for the Level 1 key skill, which are targeted quite specifically at the collection and presentation of information.

Communication (C)

Part A of the specification requires students to take part in discussions, read and obtain information, and write documents. All of these are fully covered on many occasions. Each unit starts with a series of discussion points, and the questions and Assessments require answers to be written in a variety of styles.

Working with Others (WO)

In this key skill, students must know how to plan an activity as part of a group, how to carry through the activity successfully, and how to review its success. If an opportunity is wanted to develop this key skill, it will probably be most appropriate to set up the state of the environment fieldwork (pages 86–89) as an activity in pairs or as a group, or to use the Marina for Watchet plan (Assessment 5) or Antarctic broadcast (Assessment 6) as group assessment tasks. Further opportunities include fieldwork in shopping centres or research into different uses of transport.

Improving Own Learning and Performance (LP)

Specific references to activities in the textbook and homework book are not made here, since the specification requires a more holistic view of the students' work and progress.

Problem Solving (PS)

This is perhaps the hardest of the key skills to incorporate into a Geography Programme of Study. It may be that it is better suited to maths or science, but geographers have much to offer in those departments where the course is designed to follow an enquiry-based approach. It will work best when students are carrying out practical work such as the state of the environment report (pages 86–89). This has been set up to allow students to choose the time, place and techniques that they will use. Similarly Assessment 5 (Marina for Watchet) and Assessment 6 (Hellwell Bay/Minehead) involve some problem solving with secondary resources.

WHAT STUDENTS MUST DO	EVIDENCE MAY BE GAINED WHEN STUDENTS ARE WORKING ON THE FOLLOWING TOPICS:
Application of Number	
N1.1 Interpret straight-forward information from **two** different sources. At least **one** source should be a table, chart, diagram or line graph.	• Tables (pages 5, 9, 15, 72) • Diagram (page 7) • Questionnaire matrix (page 45) • Census data (page 54) • Divided rectangles (page 57) • State of the environment report (pages 86-89) • Line graph (page 100) • Population pyramids (pages 101, 110)
N1.2 Carry out straight-forward calculations to do with: (a) amounts and sizes (b) scales and proportion (c) handling statistics.	• Car production figures (page 9) • Questionnaire results (page 45) • Shopping centre health (page 47) • Measuring width from map (page 77) • Coral reefs (page 83) • State of the environment report (pages 86-89)
N1.3 Interpret the results of your calculations and present your findings. You must use **one** chart and **one** diagram.	• Questionnaire matrix (page 45) • Divided rectangles (pages 45, 54) • Assessment score (pages 71, 75) • State of the environment report (pages 86-89)
Information Technology	
IT1.1 Find, explore and develop information for **two** different purposes.	• Design and use questionnaire for shopping survey (page 45) • Collect data for state of the environment (pages 86-89) • Research for Antarctic assessment (pages 92-93) • Research on local environment (page 90)
IT1.2 Present information for **two** different purposes. Your work must include at least **one** example of text, **one** example of images and **one** example of numbers.	• Design an advert (page 18) • Campaign literature (page 63) • Word process report on state of the environment, including use of spreadsheets and graphs (pages 86-89) • Assessment (page 38)

WHAT STUDENTS MUST DO	EVIDENCE MAY BE GAINED WHEN STUDENTS ARE WORKING ON THE FOLLOWING TOPICS:

Communication

C1.1
Take part in a **one-to-one** discussion and a **group** discussion about different, straight-forward subjects.

- Discussion points at the start of each unit
- Discussion about questions at the end of each spread could be whole class discussions, or between individual students
- A one-to-one discussion between pairs of students planning how they will collect fieldwork data on the state of the environment (pages 86–89) or shopping centres (pages 44–45), or planning the Assessments on Watchet Marina (pages 56–57) or the Antartic (pages 92–93).

C1.2
Read and obtain information from **two** different types of documents about straightforward subjects, including at least **one** image.

- Newspaper articles (pages 8, 47, 48, 84, 85, 102)
- Using an atlas (pages 57, 95)
- Letters (pages 38, 48)
- Photos and maps (pages 29, 38, 39, 56, 57, 92, 93) plus most other spreads

C1.3
Write **two** different types of documents about straightforward subjects. Include at least **one** image in one of the documents.

- Letter writing (page 17)
- Poster (page 18)
- Report (page 38)
- Plan for development (page 56)
- Campaign material (page 64)
- Postcard (page 83)
- State of the environment report (pages 86–89)
- Broadcast script (page 92)

WHAT STUDENTS MUST DO	EVIDENCE MAY BE GAINED WHEN STUDENTS ARE WORKING ON THE FOLLOWING TOPICS:

Working with Others

You must provide at least **two** examples of meeting the standard for WO1.1, WO1.2 and WO1.3 (one example must show you can work in one-to-one situations and one example must show you can work in group situations):

(See notes on page 9 on activities in pairs or in groups.)

WO1.1
Confirm what needs to be done to achieve given objectives, including your responsibilities and working arrangements.

- Plan the dates and times of collection of the state of the environment data; what data are to be collected; who is responsible for drawing up a record sheet; who is responsible for obtaining the necessary equipment, etc.; who is going to do which days (pages 86–89)
- *Plan the shopping centres to survey; who is to do each shopping centre; how to sample the people; who is going to design the questionnaire; safety arrangements, etc. (pages 44–45)*

WO1.2
Work with others towards achieving given objectives, carrying out tasks to meet your responsibilities.

- Carry out the data collection
- Offer help and support to others when appropriate
- Pass on the data collected so that others may use it

WO1.3
Identify progress and suggest ways of improving work with others to help achieve given objectives.

- Discuss the success of the activity – offer constructive criticism and advice
- Consider how the experience could help improve a similar activity next time

Improving Own Learning and Performance

You must provide at least **two** examples of meeting the standard for LP1.1, LP1.2 and LP1.3:

LP1.1
Confirm understanding of your short-term targets, and plan how these will be met, with the person setting them.

- Targets for study-based learning could apply to work over the whole year, or could apply to a particular Assessment in the light of the level of achievement reached in the preceding Assessment.
- It may be possible to set targets for activity-based learning, depending on the way the course is designed and the amount of practical work the students carry out.

LP1.2
Follow your plan, using support given by others to help meet targets. Improve your performance by:
- studying a straightforward subject
- learning through a straightforward practical activity.

LP1.3
Review your progress and achievements in meeting targets, with an appropriate person.

Problem Solving

You must provide at least **two** examples of meeting the standard for PS1.1, PS1.2 and PS1.3:

PS1.1
Confirm your understanding of the given problem with an appropriate person and identify **two** options for solving it.

- Once the state of the environment data has been analysed, suggest how the area can be improved (pages 86–89)

PS1.2
Plan and try out at least **one** option for solving the problem, using advice and support given by others.

- Carry out an improvement plan for the state of the environment activity (pages 86–89)

PS1.3
Check if the problem has been solved by following given methods and describe the results, including ways to improve your approach to problem solving.

- Repeat the state of the environment fieldwork to see if the problems have been solved and the area improved (pages 86–89)

INDUSTRY

Do the work walk!

QUESTIONS

1 Keep your eyes open on your way to school or on your way home. Look out for ten people doing different jobs. Fill in this job survey. An example has been done for you.

TYPE OF JOB BEING DONE	PRIMARY, SECONDARY, TERTIARY, QUARTERNARY	MALE OR FEMALE	TIME OF DAY, i.e. MORNING OR AFTERNOON
1 Driving a bus	Tertiary	Female	Morning
2			
3			
4			
5			
6			
7			
8			
9			
10			

2 Construct a pie chart to show the percentage of primary, secondary, tertiary and quarternary jobs that you recorded. You will need a protractor, pair of compasses, and a pencil.

If you observed ten people, then each person will equal 36 degrees because there are 360 degrees in a circle – 360 ÷ by 10 = 36.

If you have four people who were doing a tertiary job, then this would mean you need to draw an angle that is 4 times 36, which equals 144 degrees.

It is a good idea to work out the degrees for each type of job first, then check to make sure that they total 360.

You could also use Microsoft Excel or a similar computer programme to input your data onto a spreadsheet and then produce a pie chart. You could use the programme to calculate and label the percentages for each segment.

3 Do your results show the same patterns that are found for the UK (see page 5 in *Student Book 2*). List reasons to explain any differences between the figures.

4 Are there any differences between the type of jobs the men and women were doing?

5 Do you think the time of day affects the type of job being carried out?

Building a car 1

Components for the Ford Escort are made in the following countries.

COUNTRY	NUMBER OF COMPONENTS MADE IN EACH COUNTRY
United Kingdom	24
Norway	2
Denmark	1
Sweden	4
Netherlands	2
Belgium	5
France	18
Germany	21
Canada	2
USA	4
Austria	3
Spain	5
Switzerland	2
Japan	4
Italy	5

QUESTIONS

1 Use an atlas to find each country, then work out where it is on the world map and label it.
2 Now look at the number of components that come from each country. Draw a flow line from each country to the Ford factory in Halewood to show how many components come from each country.
3 Why you think some countries supply more components than others?

Drawing flow lines: a flow line is an arrow that is drawn to scale. Look at the values first. Decide on a suitable scale for example 1mm equals one component. Using this scale, an arrow drawn from Germany to the UK will be 21mm (2.1cm) thick. Make sure that the arrow points in the direction that the component is moving, i.e. the tip should be towards the UK and the rest of the line should join to Germany.

Building a car 2

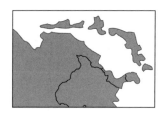

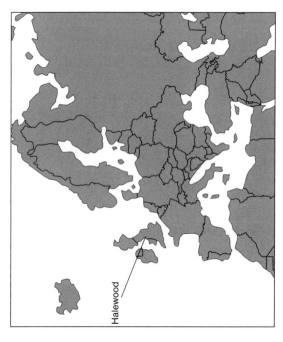

Halewood

On the buses

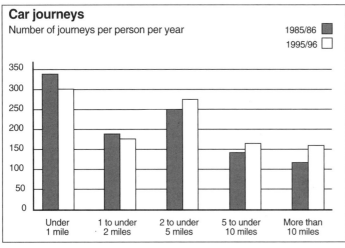

Car journeys
Number of journeys per person per year

1985/86 ▨
1995/96 ☐

A

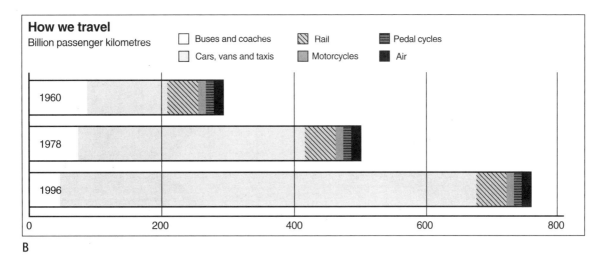

How we travel
Billion passenger kilometres

☐ Buses and coaches   ▨ Rail   ▨ Pedal cycles
☐ Cars, vans and taxis   ▨ Motorcycles   ■ Air

B

QUESTIONS

1 a Look at graph **A**. Describe what has happened to the number of journeys under 2 miles since 1986.

  b Describe how the number of journeys over 2 miles changed between 1985/86 and 1995/96.

2 a What is the most popular form of transport?

  b What has happened to the number of people using buses and coaches since 1960?

3 In 1998 John Prescott, the Deputy Prime Minister, announced his plans for creating a better transport system that did not do so much harm to the environment or people's health. He suggested the following solutions:

• Make safe routes for children to walk and cycle to school.

• Provide more bus lanes and cycle tracks and improve public transport.

• Make people pay money to enter town centres by car.

• Make people pay money (tolls) to use motorways.

• Improve rail travel and encourage more goods to be transported by rail.

• Make charges for parking where people work when public transport has been improved.

• Make sure buses and train services link together and people can find information about them easily.

a If John Prescott's plans work, what should happen to the graph showing the way we travel by 2014?

A fair cuppa

QUESTIONS

1 Café Direct recently won a contract to supply MPs with coffee at the House of Commons. Describe why you think MPs chose this particular brand of coffee. Use the information in the advertisement in your answer.

2 Now design a leaflet to persuade people to buy jewellery from Panya and Wanlee Butrachat who come from Surin in Eastern Thailand. They 'work as jewellers using traditional skills passed down from generation to generation. Thaicraft, the company they work for, guarantees them good prices and a bright future for their children'.

Left luggage

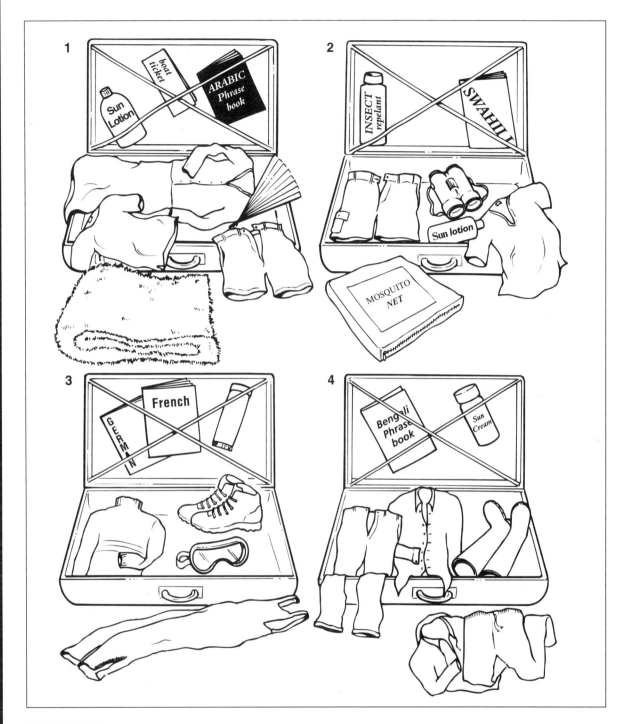

QUESTIONS

1 Suggest four countries that the people could have packed their cases to visit.

2 Draw two more suitcases. Put in them five items that might be needed to travel to Chile and Australia.

3 Choose any country visited by many tourists. Design a leaflet encouraging visitors to go to that particular country. You will need to draw a climate graph, advise visitors of the clothes they should take with them, the time of year to visit and the key attractions.

Commentary on the questions

Student Book

Industry (pages 4–5)

The discussion points explore different perceptions of work held by the students.

1 Tertiary

3 Lack of machinery prevented people from producing a worthwhile surplus. For most people if they wanted to eat, there was no alternative to producing it themselves.

4 a Students should be encouraged to make simple analytical comments (backed up by data) such as 'in Ethiopia primary work is by far the most important, but in the UK only 2% do this work'.

   b Students should use the idea that some countries cannot afford the machinery that would do much of the primary work. Other possible reasons are the UK's ability to import cheap, raw materials, or the fact that if Ethiopia's workforce does not earn much money, they cannot pay for secondary goods or tertiary services. Very astute students may raise the issue of appropriate and intermediate technology, and the issue of rural unemployment.

Making cars (pages 6–7)

1 21.

2 The cost of transporting finished cars is high. It is cheaper to locate close to the customers.

3 Antarctica, Australia, and Africa. Antarctica has no one living there apart from scientists and Africa has a lot of poor people who can not afford to buy cars. Australia has a relatively sparse population.

4 As one company sets up more arrive in the area to supply and service it.

5 The multiplier effect happens. Component factories may close down. There will be a lot of unemployment, people will have less money to spend and many of the shops and services which set up to supply the car workers may close down. Some people may move out of the area and the skilled and trained workforce may disappear. With less money coming into the area it is likely that the services provided by the council will suffer.

Cars come and go (pages 8–9)

1 a The spider diagram should be labelled.
- close to the market, the USA is the second biggest market for BMWs, so transport costs reduced;
- transportation links: deep water port, airport and road and rail systems;
- government help with cheaper taxes;
- government help in finding land and specialist training;

- suppliers close by;
- Greenfield site.

   b • cost of land;
- factories available;
- what the environment is like and facilities near the site, e.g. schools and good housing;
- the building and site can be managed sustainably;
- planners will allow the site to be used.

   c BMW wanted to build its own factory. They would have considered the cost of the land and the planning permission for the land but the State of South Carolina would have been keen to attract the factory and so even offered them cheaper taxes to move there. BMW did not have to worry about the quality of the environment to attract the workers because they were willing to apply for jobs. BMW are concerned with aspects of the environment such as distance from public transport systems such as rail. By locating in a greenfield site workers and goods will need to travel a fair distance to get to the assembly factory.

2 a USA, Canada, UK, South Africa, Columbia, Brazil, Kenya, Portugal.

   b The most efficient factories have been built during the 1980s and 1990s. However, Columbia's factory was built in 1992 but only produces 10 cars per person. It may also be more difficult for Toyota to work in poorer countries. The countries lower down in the productivity table are also a lot hotter and may have parts of the day when the workers do not work.

3 a/b BMW produces 300 cars a day. To calculate a total for the year multiply by 365 = 109,500 which is then divided by 2000. There are 54.7 cars produced by each worker. This is not quite as efficient as the Toyota factory in the USA but much more efficient than other countries with Toyota factories.

   c BMW build luxury cars and these may take slightly longer to make. It is far more efficient than the other factories because it is very hi-tech.

4 A car assembly factory can help the local community when the multiplier effect takes place.

Reduce, recycle, re-use (pages 10–11)

1 *Recycled:* pallets, the car, plastic bags, metal, water, cardboard. *Reduced:* energy emissions. *Re-used:* oil, metal, engine.

2 The lorries could use an alternative fuel such as gas or electricity. Public transport systems could be set up which connect the factory to the railway line. Larger lorries could be used less frequently. Local suppliers of components could be used more than those far away.

3 Encourage students to start with their own personal experience of transport use and to question the types of transport they use. Are there really no alternatives?

Technology in India (pages 12–13)

1 a Bangalore, Bombay and Chennai appear to be richer than the rural area of Canning Town in West Bengal.
  b Bangalore, Bombay and Chennai have attracted hi-tech industries, employment and wealth through the multiplier effect. Canning Town is very rural with few road and rail links, plus islands which can only be reached by boat.

2 Small islands with poor transport links.

3 They cannot afford expensive machines. If machines broke down, it would be difficult to repair them. The important wildlife may conflict with industry.

4 Fair trade is important because it returns as much money as possible back to the community who have made the products. It will improve people's lives.

5 SKVIS has raised standards of living. SKVIS has trained the workforce, provided them with skills and loans.

Travel the world (pages 14–15)

1 a Hawaii, Galapagos, Giant's Causeway etc.
  b Europe and Asia.
  c They are the areas which had very early civilisations and many of the world's largest populations.

2 a London to Sidney.
  b The furthest.
  More people travel by plane, so prices can be lower.

3 a The USA.
  b It earns money from other industries.

4 a USA, 42.5 million US$.
  b They are wealthy.

Stop off in the UK (pages 16–17)

2 It is nearer.

3 a Alton Towers, Madame Tussauds, Tower of London.
  b Kew gardens, St Paul's Cathedral, London Zoo, Science Museum, Natural History Museum, Tower of London, Madame Tussauds.

4 a More foreign visitors arrive at the capital city and visit close attractions. Gatwick, Stanstead and Heathrow airports are all near.
  b Public transport could provide links.

5 a Environmental: soil erosion, population, litter. Social: crime, noise, changes to the community, better buses. Economic: expensive houses, more money, more jobs, seasonal employment.

Extensions (page 18)

1 Land, good transport links, a pleasant area to live in and many good businesses.

2 a M40, railway, flat land, land for business development, pleasant environment for workers, skilled workforce close to University of Warwick and Coventry.

4 a Greenfield and brownfield sites to choose from. Components could be transported by road or rail.
  c Employment levels would rise. Loss of farmland and wildlife on a greenfield site. More traffic and more houses.
  d More cycle tracks, public transport, staff buses.

5 a Warwick Castle, Pump Rooms, Jephson's Gardens, St Nicholas Park, Warwick Race Course.
  b Most are cultural and historic attractions. The racecourse is a sporting attraction.
  c France and the rest of Europe. Older tourists who like historic and cultural attractions.
  d Traffic congestion, litter, higher prices and more tourist shops, but they will also bring money and jobs. Local facilities could be improved as a result.

6 Bisena Hali could apply to the Indian Government for a loan to start up a business. They could use appropriate technology.

Homework and Assessment Book
Worksheet 2: Building a car (page 13)

1/2 Answers on the map.

3 More components are supplied by the nearest countries.

Worksheet 3: On the buses (page 15)

1 a Decreased.   b Increased.

2 a Cars.   b It has remained constantly low.

3 a There will be fewer cars and more public transport.
  b The number of journeys by car would be reduced.

Worksheet 4: A fair cuppa (page 16)

1 The coffee is freshly roasted and a good product but it is also fairly traded and benefits poor people.

2 The leaflet should use the fair trade messages.

Worksheet 5: Left luggage (page 17)

1 Case 1 is Egypt, case 2 is Kenya, case 3 is Switzerland and case 4 is Bangladesh. Other answers which fit the bill can be accepted.

2 Chile: T-shirt, shorts, Spanish phrase book, water bottle for desert, mountain climbing equipment, Pesos. Australia: dollars, sun cream, surf board, scuba diving equipment, T-shirt, hat.

3 Students could use IT packages such as Publisher. They could do a moving advert using Powerpoint.

COASTS

WORKSHEET 6

Coastal tour

QUESTIONS

1 Which places are most likely to suffer from coastal erosion? .
Explain your choice.

2 Which places are most likely to suffer from coastal flooding?
Explain your choice.

3 Which areas do you think would be important for wildlife?
Explain your choice.

Houses with sea views

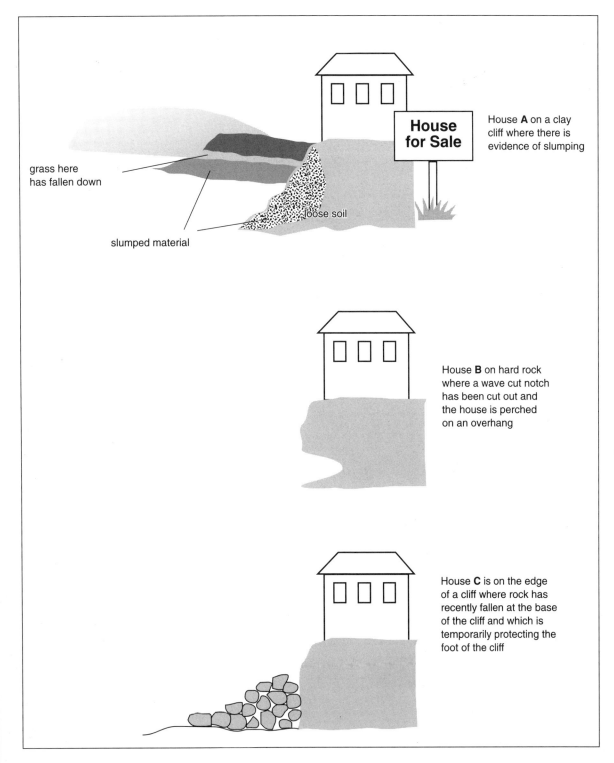

grass here
has fallen down

loose soil

slumped material

House for Sale

House **A** on a clay
cliff where there is
evidence of slumping

House **B** on hard rock
where a wave cut notch
has been cut out and
the house is perched
on an overhang

House **C** is on the edge
of a cliff where rock has
recently fallen at the base
of the cliff and which is
temporarily protecting the
foot of the cliff

QUESTIONS

1 Which of these houses do you think is in the
greatest danger of falling down the cliff after
heavy rain? Explain why.

2 Which of these houses do you think will fall
down first if rocks are hurled at the base of
the cliff? Explain why.

3 Which house will be protected for a short
while but may suffer from wave erosion later?
Explain why.

Moving along the coast

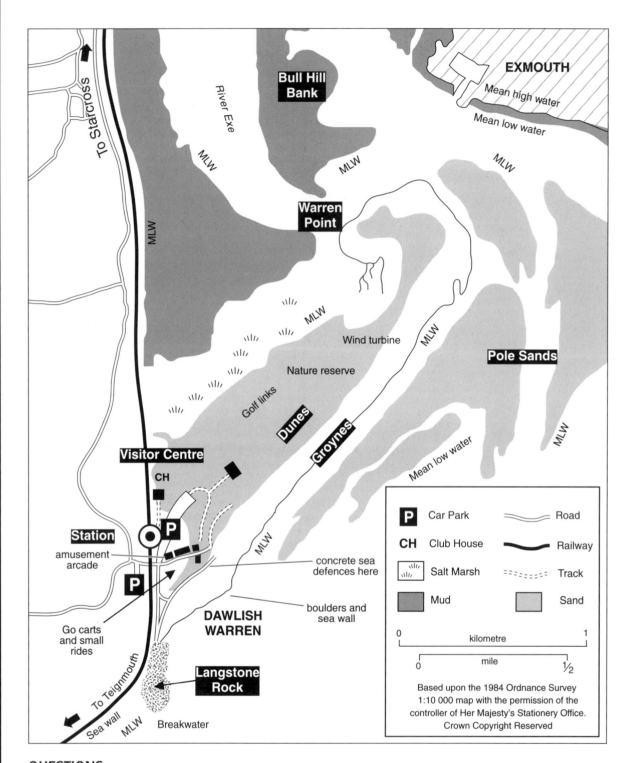

QUESTIONS

1 What is the term for this sort of coastal feature?

2 Which direction is the wind drift moving?

3 Why is the end of the feature curved?

4 What can people do here if they visit the site?

5 What management problems could be happening at Dawlish Warren?

Letting the sea through

Porlock Bay in West Somerset has a shingle bank formed of gravel that was deposited during the last ice age. Geographers who studied the bank found that the sea was eroding it. The authorities responsible for it decided that they would never be able to build the ridge back up and stop the erosion. Instead of building expensive defences they decided to use managed retreat. The sea was allowed to break a hole in the bank and now an area of marshland is gradually forming behind. During the floods the marsh vegetation and soil is able to absorb some of the extra sea water, which reduces the height of the flood waters.

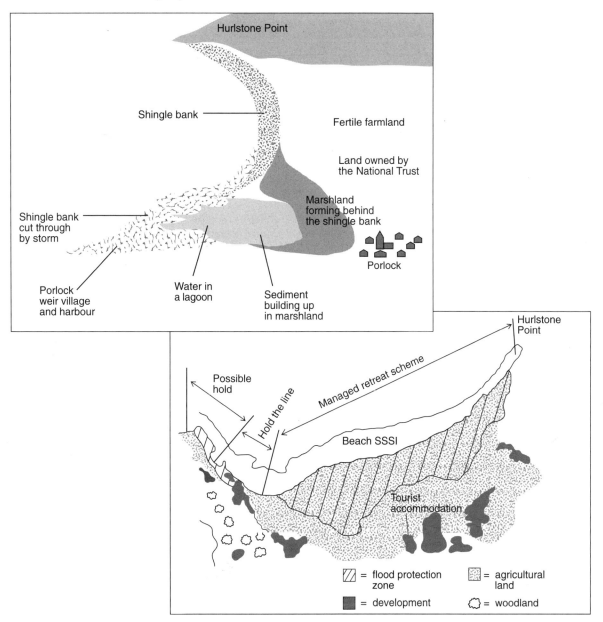

QUESTIONS

1 Why do you think that the National Trust has not tried to repair the gap in the shingle bank?

2 Who might be angry about the managed retreat scheme?

3 Who might think the managed retreat scheme is a good idea?

4 How does the managed retreat scheme work?

5 Do you think this scheme is a good idea? Give reasons for your answer.

Managing floods

QUESTIONS

1 What could you do to help stop the following flood problems? Copy the table and then write possible solutions under each heading. Some solutions may be used in more than one column.

A STORM SURGE COULD BE MANAGED BY	SEA LEVEL RISE COULD BE MANAGED BY	SINKING LAND COULD BE MANAGED BY

Solutions

1 Reducing carbon dioxide pollution
2 Encouraging people to save electricity
3 Encouraging people to use public transport
4 Building a barrier that can be shut if necessary
5 Building sea walls
6 Using managed retreat
7 Building dykes
8 Evacuating people
9 Using beach feeding to increase the width of the beach
10 Using groynes to trap sand and stones on the beach

2 Choose one solution from each heading and explain why you put it there.

Appealing for the Dee

RSPB

Turning
— the —
T i d e

A Future for Estuaries

THE DEE ESTUARY

The Dee estuary- its wildlife value

The Dee estuary, straddling the border between England and Wales, covers 31,500 acres and is one of the most famous and important places for birds in Britain.

In the summer, the saltmarshes are home to large numbers of nesting terns, redshank and shelduck, birds that nest in the marshes and surrounding fields. But it is in the winter that the Dee really comes alive. Some 82,000 wading birds spend the winter in the estuary, including 30,000 oystercatchers, 17,000 knot, 14,000 dunlin, 6,900 redshank, 6,750 lapwing and 3,400 curlew.

Threats and problems

The Dee estuary is subject to a variety of threats. The estuary's value to birds has already been greatly reduced: windsurfers, jet-skiers and walkers have caused massive desertion of bird roosting areas, which are so important to birds when the tide is covering the mudflats.

The answers

The conservation of the Dee depends upon the involvement and support of the local community. The estuary is an important local asset. Its wildlife is becoming an increasingly significant resource for tourism and recreation. But the careful co-existence of all coastal users requires careful zoning of competing needs, such as sailing and jet-skiing, in order to avoid potential conflicts and damage to wildlife. This, in turn, requires the active involvement of local planning authorities.

Only if all these measures are taken into account will the needs of birds in the Dee estuary be assured for the future.

DANGER
MAN AT WORK

The RSPB Estuaries Appeal
FREEPOST
RSPB
The Lodge
Sandy
Bedfordshire
SG19 2BR

A stamp
will save
us paying
postage

QUESTIONS

1 What problems do the RSPB want people to think about when they see the picture on the front of the appeal envelope?

2 What are the problems that birds face on the Dee estuary?

3 Design an envelope for an appeal by the RSPB to help the Dee estuary.

Commentary on the questions

Student Book

Coasts (pages 20–21)

The postcards from Aberdeen were posted in 1926. Shanklin dates from the 1920s. Bray and the Giant's Causeway is earlier, probably before 1915. Dresses are longer in this early part of the twentieth century than they were in the 1920s.

The British seaside began as a destination for wealthy Victorians. It was not accessible to everyone until the Holiday with Pay Act in the 1930s. Shanklin seems to be a residential resort, whereas Aberdeen seems to be more crowded and more casual. Bray and the Giant's Causeway look as though they are destinations for the wealthy, seeking good sea air and, in the case of the Causeway, a sample of spring water at the same time!

The fishing fleet of Aberdeen has suffered from foreign competition and over-fishing. There are fewer boats today. Today the coast is open to nearly every one not just the wealthy. The seaside is casual and people wear brief swimwear.

At Bray, the granite rocks reach the sea. This hard rock stands out as a headland and a bay has formed in the slightly softer metamorphic rock. At Shanklin, the cliffs behind the houses are made of horizontal beds. These layers of different sedimentary rocks such as sandstones and clays, have eroded to form almost vertical cliffs.

At the Giant's Causeway, basalt, an igneous rock, has cooled to form hexagonal columns of rock. The sea attacks the joints and leaves them standing as hexagons. Aberdeen has a large bay and low cliffs.

People have not changed the Giant's Causeway very much. All the other resorts have sea walls built to protect the settlement from the sea. Shanklin, Aberdeen and Bray all have a promenade. At Shanklin there is a stone groyne or breakwater. This has caused sediments to build up. It may be here to slow down the drift or to create a deeper area of bathing water.

Today promenades will have dozens of shops, cafes and cars.

2 a **Estuaries:** Exe, Tees, Wash, Humber, Thames, Solent, Severn, Firth of Forth, Moray Firth.
Headlands: Crowhead, St David's Head, Beachy Head, Flamborough Head, Dunnet Head.
Bays: Galway Bay. Morecambe Bay.
   b Chalk and limestone. They are the hardest sedimentary rocks in the south and east of Britain.
   c North and west. There is a greater variety of rocks.

3 a Tourism, fishing, industries on flat land around the coast plus good trading links.

b Shallow, nutrient-rich, ice-free waters of the British coast provide excellent food for wildlife. Estuaries are important for migrating birds.

Losing land (pages 22–23)

1 Hard, slowly, soft, quickly.

2 a Line of weakness turns into a cave. Two caves join together to form an arch.
   b Arch will collapse to form a stump, then a stack.

3 a St Gowan's Head, Worm's Head, St David's Head – igneous rock
Mumbles Head – limestone
Swansea Bay – coal and alluvium
St Brides Bay – coal and millstone grit.
   b The sea will erode this softer rock and leave the Gower as an island.

4 They wear away quickly and in some with clay, they would not form at all.

Cliffs (pages 24–25)

1 Photo **D** There is an area of exposed rocks in front of the cliffs.

2 Photo **B**, diagram 2 since it has joints in limestone.
Photo **A** on page 24 is diagram **1**, the sandstone is laid down in beds horizontally and these have formed a steep cliff.
Photo **D** on page 25 is diagram **4**, the rock tilts backwards inland.
Photo **E** on page 25 is diagram **3**. The rock has been tilted so that it is nearly vertical and the bedding planes dip towards the sea.

3 • Whether the rock is jointed, jointed rocks can be vulnerable to wave attack.
   • Rocks erode at different speeds. Layers of permeable rock over impermeable layers could result in mass movement.
   • Which way the beds lie. Vertical beds could result in landslides. Horizontal beds could lead to steep cliffs which produce overhangs.
   • Where the water reaches between high and low tide. This is the place that the waves attack the cliff. If the water does not reach the cliff, then the erosion may be caused more by rain and wind action than wave action.
   • How much vegetation covers the cliff. A dead cliff may be greener.

New land from old (pages 26–27)

1 They may have fallen from the cliff and not been attacked by attrition or corrasion yet. The rocks could be part of a storm berm where large rocks have been moved by large waves.

2 a Right to left since the sediment is piled up on the right of the groyne.

  b Shanklin. It is moving from west to east

3 You could take the following measurements:
- How stones move along a beach, to see if there is any longshore drift. Look at stones near groynes or headlands to see which way the sediment is moving.
- The frequency of waves to find out if they are destructive or constructive.
- How long it takes a pebble to travel from one end of the beach to the other by longshore drift. This may vary at different times of the year so it would be a good idea to measure it under different weather conditions.
- The angle of the beach. When sediments are building up the angle is more gentle than when erosion is taking place.
- The type of beach material. Sand will erode much more quickly than stones as they are much heavier.

Zooming in on Hampshire's coast
(pages 28–29)

1 It is an SSSI and contains information about one particular time in the earth's history.

2 b The cliff line has moved forwards, the area in the foreground of photo **D**, which had been eroded by the sea and was covered in beach deposits, is now covered by some slumped material from upslope. This appears to be at least a metre wide.

  c Water has moved through the permeable layers of sand and gravel and has then stopped where it joins the silty clay and Barton clay. All this water makes the clay sticky. The clay begins to move carrying the layers above with it. An area of soil and rock moves downslope as a slump.

  d The sea will erode the slump when there is a high tide or during a storm.

3 a Soft rock are eroded by the waves and by rain water. Permeable rock is above impermeable creates drainage problems. It also faces the Atlantic Ocean. The fetch is very big and so waves which hit the coast can be huge.

  b People have built coastal defences to the west of Barton. This has slowed down longshore drift and reduced the amount of material that is usually eroded from cliffs. Less material means smaller beaches and less protection in areas where cliffs are being attacked.

Moving and shaping: Hurst Castle spit
(pages 30–31)

1 Caravan site owner: flooding resulting in loss of income. Farmer: fertile farmland will be flooded and made salty. Birdwatcher: the marshland will be eroded and there will be fewer birds. Boat owner: there will be no sheltered mooring. Resident of Keyhaven: the sea wall may erode and flooding may occur causing damage. Fisherman/woman of Keyhaven: the spit protects boats from strong winds.

2 a Flat and marshy.

  b The land is flat and already quite wet so the water cannot be absorbed.

3 a Rock armour along the spit, sea wall, groynes and a stepped revetment at Milford.

  b Rock armour reduces the waves' energy as they hit the coast, groynes slow down longshore drift, sea walls stop the waves breaking by reflecting them back again. They also act as a barrier to high tides, preventing flooding. Revetments reduce wave energy by causing waves to break before they reach the sea wall.

4 Natural sediments which used to build it up have now been controlled further west. The amount of material taken away by currents is greater than the amount arriving at the spit, so artificial protection is necessary. The spit has extra stones added.

5 The input of sediments from the west is controlled by other sea defences. The spit cannot survive without people helping out.

Coasts of the future (pages 32–33)

1 a There are very few people.

  b Barton is not a very well known coastal resort. The coastal defences look like a building site. The beach does have some sand but is mainly pebbles.

2 Barton and Milford are bathing beaches. Jet skis are noisy but they can also be dangerous in an area where there may be people in the water.

3 Areas with housing have hold the line defences. Other areas where wildlife and geology are unimportant, or where land is not as valuable have less protection.

4 The following organisations would have been invited to the meeting:
- DOE would need to be asked about the sand and gravel needed to be added to the spit from the bottom of the sea.
- English Nature because of the wildlife interest of the salt marshes.
- Environment Agency because they are interested in flood defences.
- Harbour Authorities because moorings could be affected by flooding.
- Hampshire County Council may want to see if the management fits with their overall plan.
- English Heritage need to protect Hurst Castle.
- MAFF as farming and fishing could be affected by the change to the spit.
- New Forest District Council.

All at sea (pages 34–35)

1 a It is reclaimed land below sea level.

  b A storm surge plus double tides, the funnelling effects of the narrow gap between England and the Netherlands. Human reasons: reclaimed land and sea defences in disrepair.

  c Better weather forecasting, improved defences. Flood warning systems, reduce global warming.

2 Reclaimed land under sea level.

3 • More roads across dams means distance and time reduced between north and south of the country.

  • More freshwater has been provided for industry.

  • Nature reserves are being formed on the edges of the dams at the coast.

  • There are areas of sheltered water for recreation.

Extensions (page 37)

1 Milford Haven. It is now a protected harbour.

2 a Layers of sand and gravel lie on top of clay. This causes slumping as too much water collects on top of the clay. The slump causes a crack in the cliff top which breaks away and slides down the cliff face.

  b Very few plants and short vegetation suggests that things have been moving recently.

3 a Jetskiers are noisy, they scare away birds and fish and can be dangerous to swimmers. Dogwalkers may not be popular with sunbathers due to the possibility of dog fouling or dogs running into the sea and perhaps scaring young children.

  b Reduce these by zoning. Tell people not to walk dogs during high tide roosts. Provide pooper scoopers.

4 a Groynes.

  b As the pebbles move along the coastline, the groyne acts as a barrier and traps them.

5 a A nuclear power station: it is dangerous not to. A profitable tourist attraction such as Blackpool Pleasure Beach. A railway: it would be expensive to rebuild

  b Farmland: because the market value for this is low. Woodland: because wood is not expensive enough to justify huge expense. A few houses: these will not be worth the same amount as the defence costs. Recreation ground: this is of low value. The playground could be moved somewhere else.

6 Coastal flooding is made worse by the greenhouse effect. Everyone contributes to it and can reduce it.

Homework and Assessment Book

Worksheet 6: Coastal tour (page 20)

1 Coastal erosion would probably take place at Bournemouth, Scarborough, the Isle of Wight and Eastbourne. These are areas of soft rock.

2 Flooding would possibly occur at Southend-on-Sea and the Wash. Storm surges and the low land.

3 Wildlife will occur in all the remote locations and along the estuaries: Anglesey, Orkney, Outer and Inner Hebrides, Isle of Man, Isle of Wight, Shetland, Thames Estuary, The Wash, Mull and Skye.

Worksheet 7: Houses with sea views (page 21)

1 House one because it lies on land which slumps. This could be clay which moves when it rains.

2 House two because the undercutting will destabilise the cliff and the top will topple over.

3 House three, rocks have just fallen from a cliff and will have to be eroded before attacking the cliff again.

Worksheet 8: Moving along the coast (page 22)

1 Spit.

2 Longshore drift is moving from the west.

3 The wind may blow from a different direction. Also the currents in the estuary move the deposits.

4 Amusement rides, go carts, refreshments, and the nature reserves, swim, sunbathe, visit the visitor centre, watch trains, visit the clubhouse, sail, wind surf or jetski.

5 Conflicts between people and wildlife. Jet skiing, wind surfing, sailing or walkers may disturb birds.

Defending the railway from the sea and trying to protect the spit. The sea wall and breakwater reduces sediment flow onto the spit, making it erode. The saltmarsh in the dunes is drying out. People may trample the dunes.

Worksheet 8: Letting the sea through (page 23)

1 It is too expensive.

2 Farmers who will lose land.

3 Wildlife enthusiasts, more wildlife. Local council, Environment Agency and National Trust save money.

4 The marshland absorbs water and traps sediment which breaks the force of the waves.

Worksheet 11: Appealing for the Dee (page 25)

1 People and wildlife often conflict. Pollution, pressure for development and disturbance by commerce seem likely.

2 The Dee's disturbance is mainly due to recreation.

Assessment 4

Managing Hellwell Bay

This assessment involves students in a number of skills, map reading, photo interpretation, decision making and problem solving, map drawing and diagram construction. It will involve letter writing and report writing, using IT skills. They will use a variety of secondary evidence.

Level 3

Students write a letter which introduces a member of staff but probably does not say what his/her job entails.

The Report

- Students offer a simple description of the physical environment at Hellwell Bay. For example they identify soft rock and the fact that it is being eroded by the sea. At Minehead they identify soft rock and the fact that flooding occurs.
- Students identify a simple human reason such as the fact that Minehead is bigger. They may muddle up what is human and what is physical.
- Students may produce simple diagrams and maps.
- There is a very simplistic solution to the problem such as we will come and put some defences up for you.

Level 4

Students write a letter which introduces a member of staff and says what their job involves.

The Report

- Physical and human factors are separated accurately.
- Students describe the rock types at both locations and show this on a clear sketch map.
- They identify the link between soft rock and erosion at Hellwell. They state that this occurs when it is windy and rainy. They also identify flooding as a problem at Minehead and the link between flooding and bad weather.
- They notice the difference in expenditure between the two sites. They describe the link between the railway and protection at Hellwell Bay and the link between Somerwest World and Minehead (or Environment Agency/MAFF).
- A solution is suggested which is simplistic but possible; for example, we will put defences up if you will pay towards them.

Level 5

Students write a letter which introduces a member of staff but which says that District Councils have a responsibility to decide on coastal protection schemes but that other agencies are also involved in the decisions along the West Somerset Coast such as the Environment Agency who look after flooding.

The Report

- Students produce a well annotated sketch map which includes details about human and physical factors and has a key and title.
- In addition to the information given at Level 4, students begin to describe and explain in more detail. The physical processes that were identified at Hellwell are explained using terms such as mass movement and corrasion. The flood conditions at Minehead are linked to high tides, poor weather and flat land.
- The human factors are linked to the difference in who owns the land. They are also linked to the different roles of flood defence involving the Environment Agency and coastal protection involving land owners and councils.
- A solution is suggested which is thoughtful and well reasoned; for example, if you are prepared to pay the same percentage that Rank Organisation has given towards the cost of the scheme, then we may be able to find the rest of the money.

Level 6

Students write a letter which introduces the member of staff, the role of councils who own and lease the land, and the Environment Agency at Minehead.

Report

Students produce a detailed sketch map which has human and physical factors plus key, north point and title.

In addition to the explanations identified for Level 5, students may mention some perceptive links such as the cause of the flooding at Minehead being linked to a storm surge or the fact that erosion at Hellwell is caused by marine processes and slumping. They make a judgement that the management is not really linked to the physical problem but to the landuse dilemmas at each site. The importance of Somerwest World to the economy of Minehead has pulled in money from national government departments as well as local funding.

A reason is suggested which is thoughtful, reasoned and backed up by evidence. For example, the only reason there are any defences at Hellwell Bay is because the County Council owns the land where the railway is and leases it out to West Somerset.

WORKSHEET 12

Shopping quiz

QUESTIONS

1 What type of shopper are you? Try this quiz out on ten of your friends and family and find out what type of shopper each of them is.

1 Which of the following shops would you prefer to visit?
  a Cheap shops, street markets.
  b Shops that you know have a good reputation for the goods you want.
  c Shops in out-of-town shopping centres where the parking is easy.
  d A shopping mall where there are good places to eat and all sorts of different shops.
  e You do not have any preference at all, any shop will do.
  f A shop with a fair trade policy or one that sells organic products.

2 Which of the following best describes your situation?
  a You are on a limited budget and that means you need to spend your money wisely.
  b You will only buy things that you really need.
  c You are so busy that you don't have much time to look around shops.
  d You really enjoy shopping, it is your favourite hobby.
  e You are quite disorganised when it comes to shopping, you are not quite sure where you are going or what you are buying half the time.
  f You always buy products which will help the environment when you can.

3 When you visit a supermarket, which of the following do you do most often?
  a Only buy the supermarket own brand items or reduced goods.
  b Have a shopping list and stick to the items on it.
  c Arrive after office hours, park as close to the shop as you can and then head for the shortest queue.
  d Go for a drink in the café first, then make sure you try all the free samples on offer.
  e You go down every aisle and also spend a lot of time in the household and clothing sections. You may buy something that you don't need!
  f Look for the organic, fairly traded and environmentally friendly products first.

4 Which of the following signs do you notice first when you enter a shop?
  a Sale, reduced, half price.
  b You read the signs which tell you where everything is, i.e. labels on the aisles in supermarkets or the goods for sale on different floors in a department store.
  c Express checkout, opening hours.
  d Café, children's play area, crèche, make-up demonstrations, free wine-tasting.
  e You never read any signs.
  f GM free, organic, Soil Association approved, dolphin friendly, recycled.

What your results show.
Mainly a = Essential shopper   Mainly c = Time-pressured shopper   Mainly e = Experimental shopper
Mainly b = Purposeful shopper   Mainly d = Fun shopper   Mainly f = Environmental shopper

2 Present your results.

3 Describe and explain your findings.

Who's going to Iceland?

Bypass the shops.

For all its charms, the local bypass or 'rat-run' is probably the last place you want to spend your precious afternoon.

Now you can do your weekly shopping by phone. Simply order a free copy of Iceland's latest 'Talking Food' catalogue. Choose from over 1,100 of your favourite items, and remember all Iceland brand goods are GM free, then call us. Shop at any time, anywhere, day or night. Delivery is free, the only charge is a £4 administration fee with each order. We deliver 6 days a week (we thought you'd deserve a rest on Sunday!), at a time to suit you. Call now and shop in less time than it takes to find a parking space.

Call 0800 328 0800

Quoting code: S99CH08

For your FREE Home Shopping catalogue call 24 hours a day, 7 days a week.

Alternatively, fill in your details below IN BLOCK CAPITALS and send this coupon to:
Iceland Frozen Foods, FREEPOST (WA1521), Warrington WA4 6FB.

Code: S99CH08

Title   Mr ☐   Mrs ☐   Miss ☐   Ms ☐   Other ☐   Address

First Name(s)

Surname

Telephone (inc. STD Code)

Postcode

ICELAND
Shopping without trying

Home Shopping is available within a 10 mile radius of the store, except within the M25 perimeter where a 3 mile radius will apply. There is no minimum order value applicable. A £4 telephone administration charge is levied to all Home Shopping orders. Further offers from Iceland and other selected companies may be made to you. If you prefer not to receive such communications by post, telephone, e-mail or fax please tick this box ☐. Iceland Frozen Foods plc, Second Avenue, Deeside Industrial Park, Deeside, Flintshire CH5 2NW, United Kingdom. Registered in London No. 1107406. Registered Office as above.

QUESTIONS

1 Which type of shopper or shoppers do you think that this service would appeal to, i.e. essential, purposeful, environmental, fun, experimental or time-pressured shoppers?

2 Explain why you chose the different types of shoppers.

3 Show the advert to the people who completed the shopping quiz. Ask them if they would use

this service. Were you right about which types of shoppers would use the service?

4 Why do you think Iceland have decided to offer this service?

5 Why do you think Iceland only deliver within a 3 mile radius of the M25?

The right spot

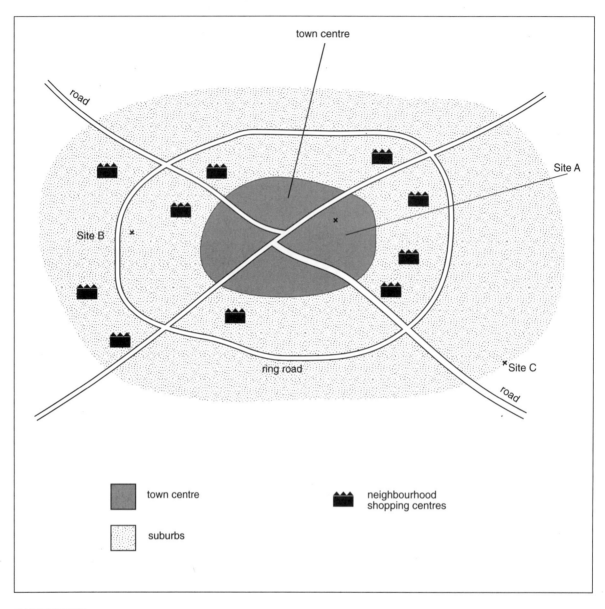

town centre

road

Site A

Site B

ring road

road

Site C

	town centre			neighbourhood shopping centres

suburbs

QUESTIONS

1 At which of the three sites would a supermarket boss choose to build
a supermarket?

2 Give reasons for the choice of location.

3 Why would he reject the other two sites?

More in store for Southam

In July 1999 the plans for the edge of town store on pages 48/49 were rejected, but a new plan was suggested to build a supermarket in the centre of Southam. Two people living in Southam wrote to their local paper:

Dear Editor,

If all that has been planned goes ahead, wouldn't it be wonderful for Southam, just the shot in the arm that Southam needs. A new supermarket, lovely, it will stop people like me going into Sainsbury's in Leamington.

All in all, the plans are to be encouraged. We would all like to see Southam bustling with people as it once was.

J McKane, K McKane, Southam

Dear Editor,

Concerning the Tesco store in Southam, we needed this store on the outskirts of town, but we were turned down because the town centre shops did not support it, so they got their way. Now they are planning to put it in the centre of town, but this will cause havoc. Car parking in the main street is chaos now. Most of the people in Southam want a Tesco store, but not in the middle of town to cause more parking problems. We have enough shop people parking on double yellow lines now. I hope the Tesco stores people go for an appeal so it can be built on the outskirts as was first stated.

TJ, Southam

QUESTIONS

1 Make two columns and label the first one good points about a new supermarket in the centre and the other bad points about the new supermarket in the centre. Use the letters to help you make a list of good and bad points under each of the headings.

2 Look at this list. Which group of people do you think would be for the new town centre store and which against it?
 • Manager of Budgens supermarket in Southam centre
 • Post office manager
 • Elderly residents
 • Car owners
 • People who rely on public transport
 • Unemployed people
 • Traffic warden
 • Young student
 • Owner of village shop in nearby village.

3 Choose one person who might be in favour of the new town centre store and one person against. Explain their point of view.

On your bike

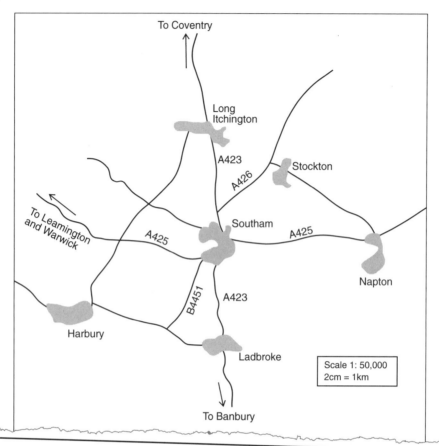

VILLAGE MOPED SCHEME

Young people in Southam, Napton, Stockton, Long Itchington, Harbury and Ladbroke are being given scooters to help them get to work or college. The County Council hopes to extend the scheme if it is successful. The Southam moped scheme is managed by the Careers Service and will provide scooters to people aged between 16 and 25 for up to ten months. The ten £1000 mopeds are being supplied by Rockinghams bike shop in Southam, who will maintain them with the Council's county fleet maintenance team. The mopeds will be allocated once the riders have been on a basic training course.

 Southam District Advertiser

QUESTIONS

1 Why are mopeds being provided for young people in these villages?

2 What types of transport could be provided to help young mothers or fathers with young children or to help elderly people?

3 Why may fewer people need to travel in the future? Make a list of the things that may allow more people to stay at home.

4 What may make commuting more expensive in the future?

The virtual village

QUESTIONS

1 Describe what is happening in this village?

2 Draw or write about what you think the village of the future will be like.

Commentary on the questions

Student Book

Shops and services (page 40)

Frequency of usage for everyday goods should come out of this discussion. Extend it further by discussing the behaviour of customers in more specialised shops. Students should be able to map out the theory themselves before they read about it.

3 'People shop in different places for different goods because some goods like newspapers are convenience or low order goods and are needed daily. They will shop for these close to where they live in their own villages or neighbourhood shopping centres. Shop keepers selling low order goods will be able to make a living because they will have many people buying items from their shops on a daily or weekly basis.

Middle order goods such as clothing will not be bought as often as low order goods and people buy them from towns or retail parks. A town has a larger catchment area than a neighbourhood shopping centre or a village and so can attract enough customers who do not visit as often.

People who need high order goods which are more specialised such as CD players travel further to buy them. These items are bought less often so shops need a bigger catchment area to make their living. Such items are found in city centres or in large out-of-town shopping centres.'

Shopping habits (pages 42–43)

2 a Clothes shops, shoe shops, antique shops.
  b If they are close together more people will visit since they like to choose items by comparing them with other shops.

3 a Chemists and doctors surgeries, estate agents, solicitors and financial services, funeral directors, florists and stone masons.
  b Customers are more likely to use a florist close to a funeral director rather than one miles away.

4 Out-of-town centres have fewer independent retailers. Large cities tend to have more shops spread over a wider area.

5 They charge high business rates and rents.

Down your street (pages 44–45)

1 Divided rectangles are easier to construct and need less equipment! You could use ICT to present the information.

2 The people who use the shopping centre are mainly female (50 per cent) from Lillington. They are all over 21 with most being over 51. People use it for daily shopping. It is close to where they live. People who work long hours use takeways and a fish and chip shop to get fast food. There is good parking to stop off on the way home. Young parents use the centre as it is accessible to buggies and has all the basic shops.

3 Students will need to design their own questionnaire and also plot the shops on a plan. They should then put their results into a matrix, present the data, describe, analyse it and present their conclusions.

Out shopping (pages 46–47)

1 a This high street appears to be quite healthy.
  b/c If the high street was not as successful, there would be more charity shops which are often given rate relief and so fill empty shops quickly. Empty shops show that business is poor as no one is prepared to locate there. One empty shop unit does not show us that the high street is unsuccessful.

3 It is likely that they do not have their own cars and so the new out-of-town shopping centres are difficult to get to.

Shopping on the edge (pages 48–49)

1 Checkout assistant, shelf stacker, trolley operative, cleaner, fruit and vegetable manager, bakery manager, restaurant manager, restaurant staff, chef, baker, butcher, marketing manager, store manager, i.e. jobs in the store. There may also be jobs linked to the supermarket, e.g. suppliers of fruit and vegetables, printing jobs, trolley manufacturers. There may also be jobs which are linked to an increase in trade, e.g. shop assistants in other shops in the town.

2 Jobs could be lost in the village shops around Southam. Some farm shops could be affected. If the supermarket has petrol, then petrol station jobs could be lost.

5 The answer must be backed up with reasons. If the person is for the decision, then expect answers such as: the supermarket will increase trade and make the centre of Southam more vibrant. It will provide more employment and will reduce prices. Arguments against it will centre on the impact that the supermarket will have on reducing trade in the centre and in outlying villages.

Community spirit (pages 50–51)

1 The villages are more like Gaydon, 86 per cent have no shop for example.

3 Try to get people out of their houses and into the community. An initial meeting could be held to decide what the people want before offering it to them. Then they need to set up some of the clubs that Harbury has. The village hall could become the centre of these activities and people could be encouraged to walk there or give each other lifts.

4 ICT: efficient transport systems could be set up and car sharing adopted if people entered details on a data base. Video conferencing could reduce travel. People could do evening classes via the computer if they had an Internet and email link to the local college.

5 Harbury could be affected by loss of trade from its village shops. This is a matter of opinion. People often use village shops because they do not have any transport or if they have forgotten items. These people would be unaffected by the superstore. Some people who shop in Harbury because it costs too much to drive to Leamington may be persuaded to shop in Southam as it is 3 miles nearer.

The rural rat-run (pages 52–53)

1 a 0.8 per cent.
  b 25.6 per cent are managers.
  c 33.3 per cent travel to Leamington.

2 Bishop's Itchington is a commuter settlement because managers generally earn higher than average earnings, most of the people work outside of the village.

3 They want better jobs and a new home environment.

4 Impacts on villages are expensive properties, reduced services.

5 Commuters could bring extra pollution, congestion and noise to towns. They could take up parking places in car parks and outside private houses.

Extensions (page 54)

1 a Out-of-town superstores competing with the shop, high business rates or rents, not a large enough catchment area, poor publicity.
  b Old aged pensioners are less mobile than other people and would need to have more shops close to them that they can reach on foot or by using public transport.
  c Lower rent, increased marketing and advertising.

2 c Crown way is not as healthy as the high street on page 47.

3 They compete with shops in the small town centres and in the outlying villages. Due to the small population, these businesses rely on the majority of local people. If these people shop elsewhere, the effect is devastating.

4 b Harbury is a commuter settlement due to a high percentage of managers, high levels of car ownership and the number that work outside the district.
  c Gaydon has fewer people working outside the district and fewer car travellers. It also has fewer managers and professional people but more technical, craft workers and machine operators. It is therefore less of a commuter settlement. Bishop's Itchington is more like Harbury.
  d Gaydon seems to be less of a commuter settlement but has fewer services than Harbury, which seems to

be more of a commuter settlement from the census data. Harbury is, however, twice the size, but it has over twice as many services.
  e Where people were born, the age of the people.

Homework and Assessment Book
Worksheet 13: Who's going to Iceland? (page 31)

1 Environmental, time-pressured, purposeful and experimental.

2 Environmental shopper due to absence of GM foods and reduced use of petrol. Time-pressured shoppers since shopping is quick and efficient. A purposeful shopper can choose exactly what was wanted in advance. The experimental shopper may use it because they have not used it before.

4 Iceland wants to increase its business.

5 There is a lot of traffic congestion around the M25.

Worksheet 14: The right spot (page 32)

1/2 a is possible because of the accessibility to all city dwellers.
  b is possible because it is on the ring road and therefore accessible with reduced congestion.
  c is possible because of the cheap land and speed of access due to lack of congestion and free parking.

3 a may be rejected because of congestion and lack of space.
  b may also be congested or have lack of space.
  c may not get planning permission because it is a greenfield site.

Worksheet 15: More in store for Southam (page 33)

1 Good points: more lively in the town and it would stop people shopping in Leamington. Bad points: increased traffic congestion.

Worksheet 16: On your bike (page 34)

1 It is difficult to get to towns to find work.

2 Buses and taxis would be more suitable, particularly ones with lifts or space to store prams, wheelchairs, etc.

3 IT revolution may encourage more home working and more Internet shopping.

4 Increases in petrol tax, road tolls and car parking tax.

Worksheet 17: The virtual village (page 35)

1 Internet shopping, home working, education via the internet.

Assessment 5

A marina for Watchet?

This assessment will contribute to achievement at Level 3 and above. When assessments 4 and 5 have both been completed this should provide fairly complete evidence of achievement at Level 3 and will contribute to evidence for achievement at Level 4 and above. For all students at all levels, this enquiry-based assessment offers not only the opportunity to use a variety of secondary sources of evidence, atlas, map and plans but also to draw maps and plans, analyse and evaluate evidence, communicate and exchange ideas, draw conclusions and be involved in decision making.

This assessment covers the following sections from the level descriptions for geography. In order to produce the final plan students may follow the processes outlined at Levels 3, 4, 5 and 6. At all levels question 2 will involve students in the use of many skills including map reading, interpretation, photo interpretation, drawing a plan, mapping skills, communication skills and decisions making. Secondary resources provide the stimulus for this. Question 1 will use atlas skills. To answer question 3 it is envisaged that students will apply the knowledge and understanding which has been learnt from previous units, notably the concepts of the multiplier effect, health of shopping centres, out-of-town and edge shopping centres, rural communities, advantages and disadvantages of tourism and types of shoppers. To get the very best from the students it may be advisable to recap or brainstorm ideas which may apply to the planning exercise. To encourage appropriate vocabulary it may be important to establish a list of words to possibly include in the answer to question 3, e.g. complementary shopping, catchment area, higher, middle and lower order goods. Students could be referred to the glossaries at the end of each unit and asked to make a list of words that could be important for this task.

Students could also be given a copy of this or a student mark scheme so that they know exactly what to aim for. If students know what outcomes are expected, they are more likely to achieve them.

For example:
- Level 3 – I can find Watchet in the atlas with some help and can describe where it is. I can draw a plan of the area and can describe the buildings I have chosen and say why I have chosen them.
- Level 4 – I can find Watchet in the atlas with some help and can describe where it is and the towns and places it is near. I can draw a plan and mark on details and give it a title and a key. I can describe the buildings and why I chose them and have some good clear reasons.
- Level 5 – I can find Watchet easily on my own. I use the index and longitude and latitude references. I can describe precisely and in detail where it is located. I can draw a plan with a key, title, northpoint and scale. I have placed my buildings carefully so that they fit the space on the map. My workshops cover about one-third of the East Wharf and I have labelled the plan carefully. I have described and explained the reasons for buildings and backed up these explanations with facts and figures from the graphs and text. I may refer to work I have learnt in units 1, 2 and 3.
- Level 6 – I can find Watchet very easily on my own from the atlas, using the index and longitude and latitude references. My plan has a scale, northpoint, title and key. I have also used symbols on my plan and have carefully placed my buildings so that they fit the space on the map. My workshops cover one-third of the East Wharf. My plan is presented very well with careful shading and labelling. I use very precise vocabulary such as catchment areas, tertiary industry, etc. to describe and explain why I chose these buildings. I use information from units 1, 2 and 3 to help me with my explanations.

Level 3

The assessment will offer students the opportunity to show their knowledge, understanding and skills in relation to the marina which is studied at a local scale. In answering question 3 they describe and make comparisons between Watchet and areas where they have studied shopping centres or industries. They should be able to offer explanations for the locations of some of the features in Watchet and they should show an awareness that different places may have both similar and different characteristics to those they have studied. They will offer reasons for some of their observations and judgements about the environment and town of Watchet and they will be able to draw a plan to show people how it could be improved for the future.

Level 4

Students begin to recognise and describe geographical patterns and will need less guidance on the concepts to apply to Watchet. They will recognise the human processes without prompting and work on a plan which will change the lives and activities of the people of Watchet. They will understand how Watchet's problems have occurred and will have clear idea of ways of improving their lives.

Level 5

Students will be able to apply many of the concepts from the unit to answer questions. So in addition to recognising shop closure as a problem they will also be able to explain why it has occurred and recognise the links and relationships which make Watchet dependent on other places. They will be able to justify their plan by representing a wide range of different views.

Level 6

The explanations will be more detailed and more convincing. There will be more empathy with the people.

Recognising levels

To mark the assessment it is recommended that teachers should award a level for each task. This will help teachers to break down levels which relate to specific parts of the programme of study.

Task 1: Find Watchet in an atlas and describe its location.

- Level 3 – finds Watchet in the atlas with assistance and describes the location in one simple sentence, e.g. Watchet is by the sea. Watchet is in England.
- Level 4 – finds Watchet in the atlas with assistance and describes the location simply but with reference to other places, e.g. Watchet is on the Bristol Channel. Watchet is near to Taunton.
- Level 5 – finds Watchet easily from the atlas, using the index and the longitude and latitude references. Describes the location more precisely and with more detail. Watchet is situated on the coast. Its closest town is Minehead. It is west of Taunton. It is near the Quantock Hills, Exmoor, etc.
- Level 6 – finds Watchet easily from the atlas, using the index and the longitude and latitude references. Introduces very precise locational information such as the distance in kilometres from the largest town Exmoor. The height of the land, the road number and type.

Task 2: Draw a plan of the site to be developed.

- Level 3 – a plan of the area with features marked on. No title, scale, key or northpoint. Workshops do not cover one third of the East Wharf site. Buildings have been placed in areas where there would not be enough room.
- Level 4 – a plan of the areas with features marked on. Title and key but no northpoint or idea of scale. Workshops do not cover one third of the East Wharf site and there are some buildings which are placed unrealistically.
- Level 5 – a plan of the area with features marked on. Title, key, northpoint and scale are all present. The workshops cover about a third of the East Wharf and the buildings are placed with care. They will fit in the places they have been put in. There is some labelling.
- Level 6 – a plan of the area with features marked on. Title, key, northpoint and scale are all present. May use symbols. The workshops cover about a third of the East

Wharf and the buildings are placed with care. They fit into the places they have been put in. The presentation of the plan is excellent, with careful shading and labelling.

Task 3: An explanation for the choice of buildings and facilities.

- Level 3 – just description of the buildings which have been planned. Reasons are given for their choice, e.g. a bingo hall is on the East Wharf because people like to play bingo. Toilets are on the Esplanade because people need to go to the toilet when they visit the marina.
- Level 4 – mainly description of the buildings but also some explanation. Much of it is limited to why they chose the buildings, e.g. they will need marina offices to look after the business of the marinas. They will need car parking for the extra tourists. A museum will be an attraction for the tourists to visit. A boat yard will be a good place for people to look after their boats. Workshops will provide jobs. More shops will give the local people better facilities. The family pub will be good for the families to visit. Guest houses and hotels will be needed for the extra tourists to stay in.
- Level 5 – writes explanations but refers to the statistics to back up the argument, e.g. workshops are needed because there is only one large employer in Watchet and there is high unemployment. Car parking is needed for tourists of whom 88 per cent use a car. Some 38 per cent of visitors are families and this is why a family pub is a good idea.
- Level 6 – writes explanations that use the statistics and also interpret them, e.g. car parking is needed for the extra tourists of whom 88 per cent use cars but there is no need for a coach park because only 4 per cent of visitors are in parties of over seven people. Building a museum may not be a good idea because only 5–9 per cent of visitors come for history or heritage. May also talk about shopping patterns and types of shoppers and how to address the problems of serving the elderly, disabled and other community members as well as the tourists. Shows thought for community members as well as tourists in the planning of the scheme. Putting a supermarket in the town may be linked to 20 per cent of people who stay in caravans and therefore self-cater but may also be sustained with local trade from residents. Uses precise vocabulary such as catchment area, tertiary industry, comparison shopping, complimentary shops.

Alternative assessment methods

This assessment lends itself to oral assessment. The plans could be produced and then individuals could present their ideas to the rest of the class. The oral assessment could then be marked by looking for the same level of explanation in an oral context.

ECOSYSTEMS

WORKSHEET 18

Know your forests

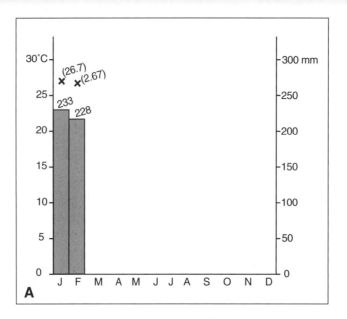

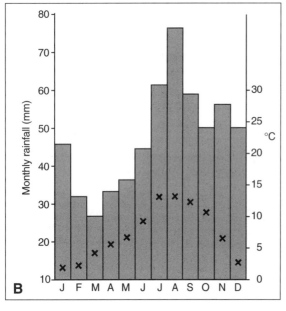

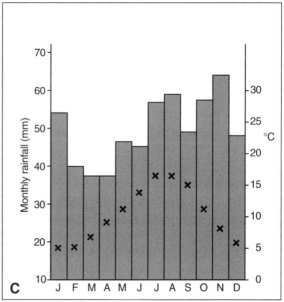

QUESTIONS

1 Complete climate graph **A** using the following figures:

	J	F	M	A	M	J	J	A	S	O	N	D
TC	26.7	26.7	26.7	26.7	26.7	26.7	27.2	27.8	28.3	28.3	27.8	27.2
R mm	233	228	244	216	177	92	55	35	51	104	139	195

2 Look carefully at the graphs and describe the three climates.

3 Match the three climate graphs to each of three forest types:
tropical rainforest, temperate deciduous and boreal. Give reasons for
your answer.

Trees that top the charts

You can estimate the age of a mature tree by measuring around its trunk at a height of one metre above the ground. Different trees grow at different rates.

NAME OF TREE	AVERAGE RATE OF GROWTH OF CIRCUMFERENCE PER YEAR IN CM
Oak	1.88
Scots pine	3.13

The wood of the trees are also very different weights.

NAME OF TREE	KILOGRAMS PER CUBIC METRE WHEN SEASONED (DRIED OUT)
Scots pine	540
Oak	720

Trees also reach full size at different times.

NAME OF TREE	AGE WHEN FULL SIZE IS REACHED
Scots pine	70–80 years
Oak	100 years but can live for over 200 years

TABLE TITLE?

NAME OF TREE	MAIN USES
Scots pine	Joinery, flooring, carpentry, general construction, packing cases, pulp, pitwood, fences, fibre board, some furniture
Oak	Furniture, coffin boards, sea defences, veneers, fences, barges

QUESTIONS

1 Estimate the circumference of the trunk of an oak planted 100 years ago.

2 Estimate the circumference of the trunk of a Scots pine planted 50 years ago.

3 If you wanted wood quickly, which type of trees would you grow?

4 Which is the heavier wood?

5 Why do you think Scots pine and oak are used for different things?

6 Measure a tree and calculate how old it is. The following list may help if it is not pine or oak: Holly (1.25 cm per year), Yew (1.25 cm per year), Beech (2.5 cm per year), Sycamore (2.75 cm per year), Spruce (3.13 cm per year).

Earthy colours

Moisture in soil is very important. It provides plants with water and moves nutrients. The soil contains dead plant and animal material called humus that helps the soil to hold water. There is usually more of this organic material where there are a large number of trees, and there is usually more organic material below deciduous broad-leaved woodlands than below coniferous woodlands.

The colours of the soil often tell us how much water is moving through the soil and how much organic material there is. Water moves minerals up and down the soil and many of these minerals, like iron, colour the soils as they move.

COLOUR	WHAT THE COLOUR SHOWS ABOUT THE SOIL
Cream	Water has taken away the iron from the soil (leaching)
Grey	A mottled bluish grey shows that there is bad drainage, i.e. the water does not move well through the soil
Red	There is a lot of iron in the soil
Orange	Some of the nutrients and minerals have been washed down through the soil
Yellow	
Light brown	
Mid-brown	The soil drains freely – water moves well through the soil
Dark brown	The soil has a lot of dead plant and animal material in it (organic material)
Dark grey-black	Good drainage – the water moves very well through the soil (sometimes it could be peat which is waterlogged)

SOIL SITE 1	SOIL SITE 2	SOIL SITE 3

QUESTIONS

1 Visit three different places close to you, such as your garden or school grounds. Use your finger to dab the soil. Try to find one of the places under a tree. Now rub the finger dab onto the soil chart above. You will have three soil colours, one in each box.

2 Write down what the soil colour tells you about the soil.

3 What do you think would happen to the amount of water in the soil if trees were cut down?

Earthy feelings

How does your soil feel? What is the soil texture? The size of the mineral particles in the soil affects how much air is in the soil and how quickly the water drains through it. A soil which is a mixture of silt, clay and sand is called a loam. These are the best types of soil for growing things because they contain the advantages of each texture.

	SAND	SILT	CLAY
Size of particles	Large – more than 0.2mm	Between 0.02mm and 0.002 mm	Small – 0.002mm and smaller
Air spaces	Large	Medium	Small
Drainage	Very quick, leaving a dry soil	Fairly quick, leaving a well balanced soil	Slow, leaving a wet soil
Temperature	Heats up quickly when it is warm weather and cools down quickly in cold weather	Does not change very quickly	Does not change quickly but wet clay can be cold
Minerals and nutrients	Washed out by the rain	Stay in the soil but not as safe as in clay	Are attracted to clay and stay in the soil

A

pH

This is a measure of how acid the soil is. It is the most important chemical information. It affects the type of plants that grow and how the soil is formed.

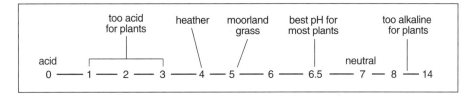

QUESTIONS

1 a Find a sample and rub it between your fingers. If it feels gritty, then it is a sandy soil. If it feels smooth but will not stick together to form a ring, then it is a silty soil. If it sticks into a sausage shape or ring, then it has a lot of clay in it.

   b Look at table **A**. Write down what will happen to water draining through your soil sample, how warm or cold the soil can be and what you would expect the nutrients and minerals to be like.

2 Why do you think it is important for gardeners to test the pH and texture of the soil before they begin to plant seeds?

3 Which type of soil do you think would be the best one to grow things in? Give a reason for your choice.

Spot the difference

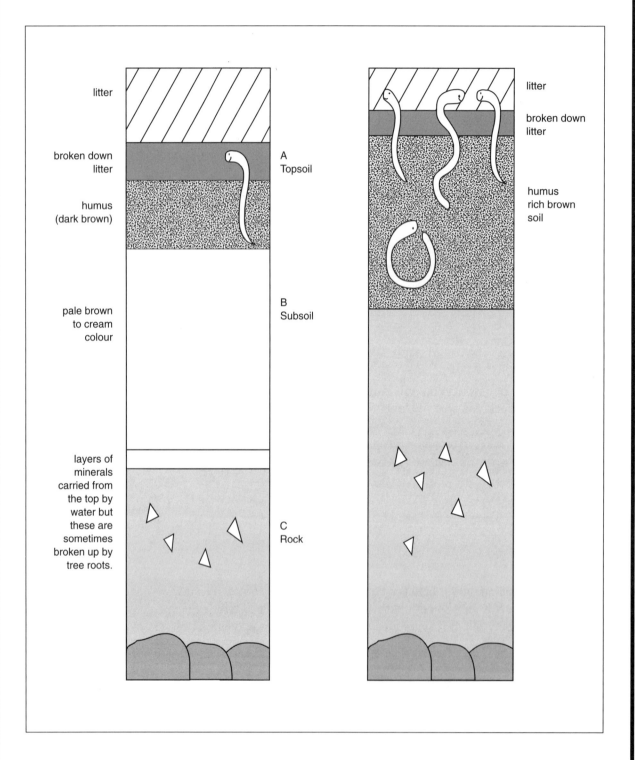

QUESTIONS

1 What are the differences between these soils? Describe the differences between the depth of the layers, what the different layers are like, and the creatures that live in each soil.

2 Which soil is found under a deciduous wood and which is found under a coniferous wood?

3 Explain your choice.

       Nelson Living Geography Homework and Assessment Book 2 © Dobson, Sander and Woodfield. Nelson Thornes. 2001

Forests forever

Rainforests have been used for thousands of years by native peoples. The Dyaks have used the Borneo rainforest sustainably for rattan and everything they needed for their everyday lives, but many other people have used them for timber and other products.

RAIN FOREST USE	DETAILS	WHERE THEY SELL THE GOODS	DISADVANTAGES
Craft items, e.g. bilum bags made from tulip tree bark in Papua New Guinea	Craft items are made from sustainable bark e.g. bilum bags made from tulip tree bark in Papua New Guinea	Tourists who visit and overseas	
Rubber	Harvesting the rubber of individual trees	In the country and overseas	Rubber plantations can harvest more rubber more cheaply so a good price is hard to get
Brazil nuts	Brazil nuts are harvested from individual trees	In the country and overseas	Brazil nut trees cannot be grown in plantations because rainforest bees are needed to pollinate the trees. Sometimes the crop can fail and collectors do not make a very good living from them. The price can vary quite dramatically
Brazil nut oil, e.g. Kayapo Indians in Brazil make this product	It is used in beauty products	Overseas	Made for the Body Shop and therefore it needs customers to want it
Fruit trees, e.g. the Awa Indians of Ecuador have done this	Some small-scale planting of fruit trees can take place within the forest	In the country	
Eco-tourism	Learning about the rainforest, small-scale trekking and undertaking conservation work	Sold a holidays overseas	Must not be too many people, buildings, airports or roads or pressure could become too much
Wax and honey, e.g. bee-keeping in NW Zambia	Using the rich insect life for economic advantage	Overseas	
Medicines	Rainforest communities should have the rights to medicinal plants found in their forest	Overseas	
Animal trapping, hunting and the wild bird trade	Animals are caught and exported for medical science (chimps) or collections or pets	Overseas and in the country	Rare species are protected under CITES. Much illegal trading takes place

QUESTIONS

1 Choose five ways of using the rainforest that you think would be of greatest benefit to both the local people and the environment. Explain why you chose these five.

2 Choose five ways of using the rainforest that you think would not be as good. Explain why you chose these five.

3 Choose one method of using the rainforest that would benefit local people and the environment and design a poster encouraging local people to use the forest in this way.

Commentary on the questions

Student Book

Ecosystems (page 58–59)

Questions of survival should start discussions about extemes of climate. Rainforest plants have waxy shiny leaves and pointed tips for the rain to run off. Cacti and camels store water in their bodies. Some desert animals and plants have long times of dormancy and only breed when the rains come. Many animals are nocturnal and come out in the cool of night. Some desert animals feed on very dry grain, e.g. gerbil. Blubber helps Antarctic animals to survive the cold. Some fish have anti-freeze in their bodies. Lichens are low to the ground and do not need soil to survive. They grow slowly and absorb nutrients from precipitation.

People have cut down rainforests. Students may be aware of the hole in the ozone layer or the Antarctic Treaty. Deserts are increasing due to soil erosion. Damage is caused by the oil industry and by agriculture. Desert soils are very fertile because so little water moves through them. People have tapped reservoirs of underground water and are using these to irrigate the soil.

1 a The hot desert areas of the world include: Atacama in South America; Mojave, Sonoran and Great Basin in North America; Sahara, Libyan, Nubian, Kalahari and Namib in Africa; Denakil, Rub-Al Khali, Arabian and Iranian, Syrian, Caragum, Qyzyqum, Takla Makan, Gobi, Thar in Asia; Simpson, Great Victoria, Gibson, Great Sandy in Australia.
   Most deserts are in the middle of continents away from moisture bearing winds of the sea or are where there are cold off-shore currents which cause fog and mist to form over the sea and prevent moisture from being carried landwards. The main belts of deserts are near the Tropics of Cancer and Capricorn.

2 a Deserts have very high temperatures, by day as high as 55°C, and less than 250 mm of rain each year. At night the cloudless skies allow heat to radiate back into the atmosphere giving temps near to freezing at night.
   b Plants have the same type of adaptation because they experience similar climates.
   c They all have ways of reducing evaporation and trapping water with extensive root systems.

3 Some biomes have already almost totally disappeared such as temperate deciduous woodlands in their natural state. Savannas are thought to be semi-natural due to actions of early people. Rainforests are most threatened now.

Tropical rainforests (pages 60–61)

1 a Light decreases downwards.

   b The tallest and largest plants are in the upper canopy layer. As you move down trees get smaller and are a pointed shape to find the narrow bands of sunlight between the larger trees. Lianas and epiphytes live off other plants, so do not need as much light. Few plants on the floor are adapted to less light.

2 Feeding by night means that they will not compete for the same food as the day living creatures.

3 The smallest creatures are decomposers. They provide food for the rainforest trees by breaking down dead plants and animals and changing them back to nitrates.

4 The nutrients in rainforests are stored in the plants themselves not in the soil. Heavy rain is likely to wash the nutrients from the surface. Crops could be planted underneath a canopy of trees, or extra fertilisers would need to be added continually. The person could move when the fertility reduces.

The world on fire (pages 62–63)

Disadvantages: lost income, wildlife killed, smog.
Advantages: it cleared land for oil palms.

2 Rich companies who plant oil palms on rainforest land benefited. They blamed the fires on El Niño. Many asthmatics were poorly. People who worked in tourism saw lost money. Orang-utans driven to the forest edge were killed for meat by poachers.

3 Pictures of orang-utan can be found on the internet.

Money grows on trees (pages 64–65)

1 a Transmigration in Kalimantan, Dyak people.
   b In Kalimantan the cleared acid soil was unsuitable for growing rice. The Dyak people were forced off their land by loggers and unable to harvest rattan.

2 The local people were against the logging and they could have explained a sustainable way of managing the rainforest.

3 The rainforest should be managed sustainably. Poor people should be helped because they are destroying the rainforest. Move the transmigrants to places where they can survive. Develop ways of managing timber which do not harm the forest.

Temperate deciduous forest (pages 66–67)

1 b The trees shed their leaves in winter to stop the water evaporating. Bark keeps them warm. Creatures become dormant or hibernate when it is cold.

2 a Oak, birch and willow attract most insects. More insects mean more food for birds and mammals.
   b Spruce, fir and larch because they have few insects.

3 a Agriculture, urban land and grassland.

b Nutrients are mainly stored in the soil and there is less rain to wash them away.

Shaping woods (pages 68–69)

2 Woodland, footpaths, wildlife, peregrine falcons, watersports, cycling.

3 a A well designed car park which fits into the woodland, toilets and refreshments.

b They could re-plant the paths, or guide water away.

Boreal forests (pages 70–71)

1 a Grow fast, soft, few, dark.

b Slowly, hard many, light.

2 The trees would not be straight enough.

3 More insects and therefore more birds and mammals.

b They grow faster and make more money.

Extensions (page 72)

1 a Deciduous woodland has less acidic soil, less leaf litter, more mini-beasts, a silty clay soil, is wetter, lighter (although the light level gets lower nearer the ground), has more plants and more gaps in the canopy than the coniferous forest.

b • Bigger gaps in the canopy let more light through. Extra light allows more plants to grow on the ground. More rain also comes through these gaps and makes the soil wetter. More plants mean more mini-beasts. Less acid soil encourages earth worms which mix up the layers of the soil. They move any decomposed leaves down into the deeper soil. Leaves decomposing quicker give a thinner layer.

• The coniferous trees have a dense canopy with very little light or rain coming through at all. This means few plants can grow underneath. Few plants mean few mini-beasts. There are fewer mini-beasts to decompose the litter which builds up. The acidity of the soil discourages the earth worms who would normally mix up the soil layers.

2 The pine needle has a thick waxy skin and sunken pores which stops evaporation. It can survive when the roots cannot get any water due to the frozen ground. Broadleaves are good for trapping sunlight in summer but shed them in winter to stop losing water. Rainforests trees have waxy surfaces and drip tips to encourage run off and stop the trees becoming weighted down.

3 a There are forest fires all over the country.

b It can contribute to the greenhouse effect. Winds blow smoke to areas away from the source of the burning. It causes economic chaos, which may affect stock markets. The loss of the rainforests reduces oxygen. There may also be micro-climatic changes which happen as a result. More smoke causes more clouds and more rainfall.

4 b Climate.

c Tropical rainforests are the hardest to manage. Nutrients are stored in the vegetation not in the soil. They are in poor areas of the world where it may mean the difference between life and death for a poor family.

d Temperate deciduous forest because there is only one area of the world in Poland where the forest has not suffered from the effects of people. Native boreal forest in Scotland because only 25 per cent of the amount available in 1957 was still there in 1990.

5 a Bluebells in temperate deciduous forest in British Isles: bluebell woods are quite rare throughout the world. They are only found in European temperate deciduous woodland. Orang-utan tropical rainforest in Indonesia. The number of orang-utan has declined as the amount of rainforest has disappeared. Bialoweizka forest in Poland. It is a UNESCO reserve where people and wildlife are cared for together. Scotland Nature reserves, money given as grants to persuade people to plant Scots pine. Pine forests should be fenced from sheep to allow natural regeneration.

A tropical rainforest. Termites are the only insect which can eat wood.

6 The sheep will prevent the forest from regenerating.

Homework and Assessment Book
Worksheet 18: Know your forests (page 40)

2 A is a tropical forest, **B** is temperate and **C** is boreal. The tropical forest has continuous constant temperature which is high and continuous high rainfall. The other two have seasons but the temperate deciduous forest has a longer summer and shorter winter which is not as cold.

Worksheet 19: Trees that top the charts (page 41)

1 188 cm. **2** 313 cm. **3** Scots pine. **4** Oak.

5 Heavier wood for strength such as sea defences.

Worksheet 20: Earthy colours (page 42)

3 More water will reach ground if trees are removed.

Worksheet 21: Earthy feelings (page 43)

2 Some plants need different pH. Texture affects how quickly soil heats up and how many nutrients the soil contains.

3 Loam soils are best due to a balance of textures.

WORKSHEET 24

Building in style

Exmoor National Park has a set of building guidelines to follow to make sure that the character of the local area is kept for future generations to enjoy.

The area where you live may already have some guidelines for it. You could try to find out if they exist. Is there a conservation area? Are there listed buildings? Do you live in a national park?

The illustrations below could help you with the questions following.

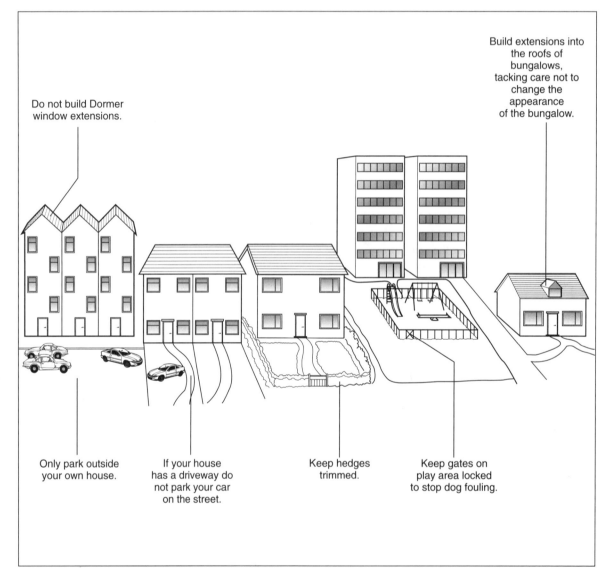

Do not build Dormer window extensions.

Build extensions into the roofs of bungalows, tacking care not to change the appearance of the bungalow.

Only park outside your own house.

If your house has a driveway do not park your car on the street.

Keep hedges trimmed.

Keep gates on play area locked to stop dog fouling.

QUESTIONS

1 Make some sketches of the houses in your street. Label the sketches to show the features that you like and the features that you do not like.

2 Use these sketches to write down a list of planning regulations you would like to introduce for your street, i.e. the things that people must do and the things that you do not want people to do.

An eco-tourism paradise?

Exmoor National Park Authority is trying to improve the area's sustainability to make sure it will still be an attractive place for future generations.

COLUMN 1 WHAT HAPPENS ON EXMOOR	COLUMN 2 A CHECKLIST FOR ECOTOURISM DESTINATIONS
A Businesses display collection boxes, place donation envelopes in hotel bedrooms or add an extra few pence to charges for food or accommodation to donate to the Exmoor paths partnership which helps to repair paths	1 Looking after the landscape, wildlife and cultural heritage
B Some businesses organise special interest conservation breaks to help keep Exmoor special	2 Efficiency of fuel and heat 3 Waste disposal and recycling 4 Using goods and services provided by local communities
C People who stay on Exmoor are encouraged to make a donation in the National Park Visitor Centres to spend on repairing paths	5 Sympathetic building and architecture
D A newsletter about the paths partnership is produced and people can subscribe to this for £5 a year	6 Educate everyone before, during and after their stay. Encourage moral and ethical behaviour
E A group of businesses called the Exmoor Producers Association encourage people to buy products made on Exmoor	7 Encourage everyone to notice the resource they are visiting
F Post offices and village stores also act as tourist information offices for the National Park	8 Make everyone work together to look after the resource
G Extra buses will run during the summer months along the main coast road to encourage people not to use their cars	9 Allow people to participate and inspire them
H The National Park Authority makes all of its visitor signs from its own woodlands, which are managed for conservation	10 Accept that the resource may limit the number of visitors to it. Develop long-term benefits to the community
I The rangers run a programme of guided walks and activities, many of which inform people about the wildlife	
J Charcoal will also be produced to provide fuel for the tourists who visit	

QUESTIONS

1 Read column 1. Read column 2. Now match the numbers from column 2 to the letters in column 1 where you think that Exmoor has achieved one of the ecotourism aims. You may use numbers more than once.

2 Decide whether you think Exmoor is an ecotourism destination or not. Explain your decision.

Behaving sensitively

The government has set up an Environmentally Sensitive Area on Exmoor. This means they will pay farmers to look after the land to protect wildlife and landscape. Farmers apply to take part in this scheme, and in return for the payment they must carry out various tasks on their land. Table **A** shows the range of habitats on Exmoor and how much money a farmer can receive.

EXMOOR ESA LANDUSES	AMOUNT PAID IN £ PER HECTARE
Owning any land in the ESA boundary	14
Improving permanent grassland (land which has had fertiliser on it in the past)	18–27
Keeping low input permanent grassland (land with less fertiliser added to it)	
Keeping enclosed unimproved permanent grassland (areas with hedges around them where no fertiliser has been added)	30
Keeping land as moorland	34
Keeping heather moorland and coastal heath	50
Planning to change the land back to heather moorland	225
Continuing to graze the purple moor grass areas	10
Making sure there are fewer cattle and sheep grazing on the moors in early winter	5
Making hedges stockproof so that animals cannot get through them	2.4 per 10 metres per hectare
Mending and planting hedges	10 per metre
Keeping land as woodlands	100
Making sure the public can visit the land	170

A

QUESTIONS

1 Look at table **A**. List the five types of land use which will give the farmer the most money per hectare.

2 a Which type of land use do you think is the rarest habitat on Exmoor?

 b How can you tell?

3 Why do you think that the farmer will be paid to reduce the number of cattle and sheep grazing in early winter?

4 Why do you think it is important to keep hedges well looked after?

5 Why is public access so important on Exmoor?

El Niño

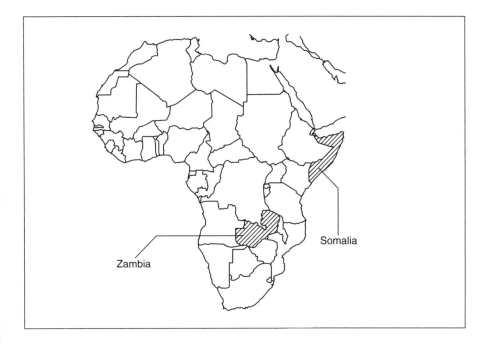

Zambia

Somalia

Victims of the El Niño environmental catastrophe in New Guinea have been reduced to eating leaves to survive. Over a million people – a quarter of the island's population – are thought to have suffered as a result of the drought caused by El Niño.

Meanwhile, in Zambia torrential rains wiped out crops and forced people to eat wild roots until they too became too waterlogged to consume, and in Somalia, 2,000 were killed by floods. The financial cost to the countries has been estimated at £10 billion.

Approximately every eight years El Niño stirs, changing the direction of ocean currents flowing across the Pacific. Dying sealife and dramatic spot flooding are the immediate signs in Peru, the home of El Niño, but the knock-on effect causes catastrophe across the Southern Hemisphere.

PLACE	PROBLEM
A New Guinea	1 Sealife dies because cold currents have disappeared and they no longer bring nutrients with them
B Somalia	2 Rainforests are very dry and burn very easily
C Zambia	3 People are suffering from drought
D Peru	4 Warm winds carrying more moisture arrive and cause flooding
E Indonesia	5 Extra nutrients carried by cold water are producing more algae on the surface that is killing the coral reefs because the sunlight cannot reach the algae in the coral itself

QUESTIONS

1 Match the problem to the place. You may use numbers more than once.

2 What could be done to help the people of Peru and Somalia and Zambia in El Niño years?

3 What could be done to help in New Guinea and Indonesia to reduce damage?

Caring for Tanzania's reefs

QUESTIONS

1 Tanzania's tourism industry is increasing very quickly. All along its magnificent coastline there are coral reefs. You have been asked to write a green code to leave in hotel bedrooms for the care of coral reefs. Make a list of things that people should not do around the reefs. Produce it in an attractive way so that people want to pick it up and read it.

2 What other things would the government of Tanzania have to do to make sure that the coral reefs survive to continue to attract the tourists?

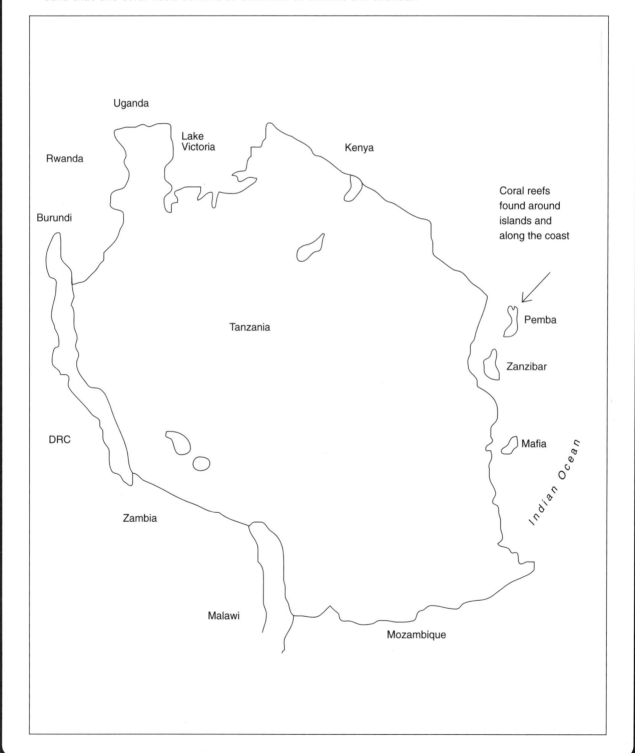

Linking lichens

Facts about lichens

- Crusty lichens grow 1mm or less per year, while leafy or shrubby lichens can grow a few cms in a year.
- Lichens can start growing again in an area within five to ten years following a fall in pollution levels.
- Sulphur dioxide and nitrous oxide dissolve in rainwater to form acids. If an area has high levels of rainfall lichens are more likely to suffer from sulphur dioxide pollution.
- Ash and willow trees have a higher pH than other deciduous trees and they are not as badly affected because they neutralise the pollution. Their bark also holds more moisture. Lichens colonise these species first when air pollution falls.
- Oak will not become colonised as quickly because the bark is acidic.
- Lichens are also sensitive to fluoride pollution (from aluminium smelting, brick works, glass milling, fertilisers, phosphorus and volcanoes). This type of pollution often causes lichens to change colour – some turn red, while others go black and die.
- Valleys often become more polluted than higher ground.
- Man-made substances like pavements and bricks are often alkaline (a higher pH) and this helps to neutralise the pollution, allowing lichens to move further onto towns.

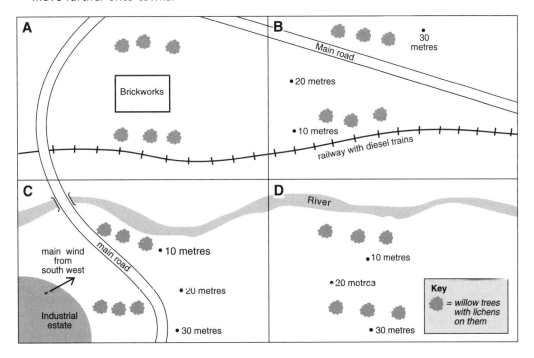

QUESTIONS

1. In which three of the four areas shown on the map would you expect to find lichens that will survive in polluted areas?

2. What would cause the pollution in each of the three areas?

3. How do types of pollution affect the growth of the lichens?

4. Which lichens would you expect to find in the fourth square?

5. Why is it sometimes difficult to compare results for lichens?

Commentary on the questions

Student Book

Environmental issues (pages 74–75)

Horse riding, walking, visiting historic sites, walking dogs, paddling or fishing in water, visiting the beach or possibly climbing. Conflicts with tourists, dogs and sheep dog faeces, traffic congestion, litter, trampled vegetation, parking problems for local residents.

Red light for Dunster (pages 76–77)

The map used on this page is 1:5000. Dunster takes up four 1 km grid squares on a 1:50000 map. A six-figure reference will take it down to a 100 metre square on the land. On the map of Dunster grids are drawn on. The grid references being used refer to the whole 100 by 100 metre square. To pinpoint houses, an eight-figure reference would be used.

2 a High Street varies from 20 metres to 40 metres. Church Street is 10 metres most of the way along but there is a narrow part which is only 8 metres wide.
  b The car would be 1 metre away from another car in Church Street at its narrowest point and 3 metres at its widest point. In the High Street the cars would be 13 metres away from each other at the narrowest place and 33 metres away at its widest.
  c Large vehicles such as coaches and lorries.
  d The High Street is wider.

Living Exmoor style (page 78–79)

1 The house has thick walls and small windows because it is cold and windy on the moor.

2 National Park Authority keeps Exmoor looking nice.

More moor (page 80–81)

1 Trampling has removed vegetation. The soil is no longer held together by the roots of the plants. The peaty soil is quickly eroded away. Finally pieces of the rock below show through the soil.

2 Various paths and bridleways all meet at this place.

3 The channel is now a deep gully and looks like a river channel, where water has meandered. There are stones at the bottom of the channel where water has passed. The path alongside has fewer stones showing so it looks as though the path has been saved.

4 'Moor care less wear' means look after the moorland habitat and do not trample it and wear it away.

Living rock (pages 82–83)

1 0.2–0.4 cm per year.

2 The water temperature needs to be 18°C.

3 a The reef contains many species of fish and coral. 9–10 million fishermen earn their living from it. 100 countries rely on tourism based on the reefs Reefs protect coastal areas from wave attack.
  b Corals live with single-celled plants. The plants give the corals nutrients in return for protection and CO_2. The corals are the base of the ecosystem.

Reefs at risk? (pages 84–85)

1 a Labels: fertilisers, boat anchors, walking on reefs, sub aqua diving, cutting down trees, El Niño, soil erosion, oil from rigs, burning forests, global warming, thermal pollution, sewage, overfishing, dredging for minerals, collecting animals.
  b Global warming is the most important since it is affecting the reefs.

2 One theory is that the sea is too warm and this forces the single-celled plants out of the coral and the coral cannot get any nutrients and then dies. The other theory is that the cold water is bringing more nutrients which are causing plankton to grow. This blocks out the light and the plants in the coral can not photosynthesise.

3 The article from the *Independent* says that nature has had the greatest effect through global warming since it has affected the reefs. However, global warming is caused by humans so people have affected this.

The state of your environment (pages 86–87)

1 • Does the quality of the school environment change with distance from the building?
  • Does the quality of the school environment vary in the school grounds?
  • Is litter the only problem in the school grounds?
  • How much wildlife is there in the school grounds?
  • Does the litter decrease with distance away from the canteen?
  • Does the landuse surrounding the school grounds have any affect on its environment?
  • Are the areas that most people use in the grounds the areas of the best environmental quality?
  • What different types of pollution are there in the school grounds?
  • Do the areas that people think are the best really the ones of the highest environmental quality?

2 Students may list the things which have been mentioned in the book, e.g. smell, noise, trampling. They may add measuring wind speed and direction to link it to CO_2 levels or litter distribution. They use soil infiltration tests to trampling.

3 Equipment is largely based on charts. A quadrat can be made out of tent pegs and string. To measure wind direction, a ribbon tied to bamboo can work. You may

need to provide sellotape and equipment for sampling the pond water if you have one.

4 One way of sampling is to provide students with an acetate sheet with numbered grid squares on it. This is placed over a base map of the school site. Ask them to choose numbers. It could be gathered in one go, or staggered over a few lessons. This exercise also lends itself to a cross-curricular approach with the science department.

Exploring living things (pages 88–89)

1 b Presentation suggestions
   - Method 1: work out the scores for the results. Decide from the results which areas are poor, in-between and good environments. Colour code some maps, e.g. red = poor environments, amber = in-between, green = good environments. Each measurement could have different colours to show the results for different areas. Overlays could be produced to show different areas.
   - Method 2: mean scores could be calculated for various indicators for the school as a whole, e.g. mean CO_2, mean trampling score, smell, noise, bird song, number of invertebrates, environmental assessment scores.
   - Method 3: each different site could have a bar chart produced from it with all the mean scores. All the bar charts could be compared.

Extensions (page 90)

2 a 1:50000: class of road, National Trust ownership, contours, ancient monuments
   b 1:5000: buildings.

3 Suggestions: use public transport, do not drop litter, shut gates after you, keep dogs on leads, clear up dog mess, buy local products, keep to the paths.

4 Heather moorland is a globally threatened habitat and can disappear when overgrazing occurs. This has happened on Exmoor and when it does bracken appears. Bushy lichens tell us that the air is not polluted.

5 Cutting down timber causes rapid soil erosion if burning leads to acid waste being washed in to the sea. The acid kills corals directly and the soil stops the sunlight from reaching the plants in the coral and they die. This is called coral bleaching.

6 Coral can encourage tourism or help to prevent coastal erosion by dissipating wave energy.

7 Sewage from the hotel will go into the sea and add nutrients. Upsetting the reef's balance. The hot water may warm the sea forcing the plants out of the coral and cause coral bleaching. Reef walking, anchoring of boats and snorkelling could break off parts of the reef. Spear fishing with poison tips can harm many of the creatures. Buying souvenirs encourages a trade in

gathering living and non-living reef materials affecting its chance of survival.

8 The lichens show pollution as the wind would blow the pollution across the grounds.

9 a Stonefly show water quality, lichens air quality.

10 Local authority and the Environment Agency are useful sites.

Homework and Assessment Book

Worksheet 25: An eco-tourism paradise? (page 49)

2 Yes: it has tried to address many of the ecotourism criteria. It also has a policy to have sympathetic building and architecture.

Worksheet 26: Behaving sensitively (page 50)

1 Moorland, woodland, public access, unimproved pasture, heather moorland.

2 a Moorland.
   b More money is given to farmers for this.

3 The stock will trample the moorland and will damage it.

4 Landscape value, stock control and wildlife value.

5 The National Park aims to encourage recreation and enjoyment of the countryside.

Worksheet 27: El Niño (page 51)

1 New Guinea, 3,2; Somalia 4; Zambia 4; Peru 1; Indonesia 5, 2.

2 a Extra food supplies in the country, alternative forms of income which are not dependent on farming or fishing, flood management schemes.
   b Fire precautions and water storage facilities.

Worksheet 28: Caring for Tanzania's reefs (page 52)

2 Reduce pollution to avoid increases in nutrients. Hotels would have to manage their sewage. Minimise destruction of vegetation which could release more nutrients into the system.

Worksheet 29: Linking lichens (page 53)

1 Lichens A, B, C.

2 A: roads, brick works, rail. B: road and rail. C: industry and road.

3 They absorb dissolved pollutants.

4 Lichens which indicate less pollution.

5 If lichens colonise alkaline surfaces such as concrete, this can be a buffer to pollution.

Assessment 6

Frozen assets

This assessment develops skill at all levels such as photo-interpretation, data interpretation, working in groups and communication skills. It provides an opportunity to assess students orally.

Tasks one and two assess at all levels the understanding of how Antarctica affects lives. At Level 3 students offer descriptions of the advantages and disadvantages of tourism in Antarctica. They recognise that it has a different physical environment to other places they have studied. They offer reasons for the views that their characters have.

Level 4 students recognise and describe human processes occurring in Antarctica. They begin to show understanding of how these processes can change the features of places, and that these changes affect the lives and activities of people living there. They show understanding of how people can both improve and damage Antarctica and they explain the different views held by people about tourism.

Level 5 students describe and begin to offer explanations for patterns and for a range of physical and human processes which affect tourism in Antarctica. Students recognise some of the links and relationships which make Antarctica dependent on other countries. They offer explanations for ways in which human activities affect the environment and recognise the different ways that people attempt to manage Antarctica in a sustainable way. They select information and sources of evidence, suggest plausible conclusions and present their findings.

Level 6 students describe and explain a range of physical and human processes and recognise that processes interact to produce distinctive characteristics of Antarctica. They describe the ways in which processes, operating at different scales, create geographical patterns and lead to changes in Antarctica. Students appreciate the many different links and relationships which make places dependent on each other. They recognise how conflicting demands on the environment arise and they describe and compare different approaches to managing environments. They select and make effective use of a range of skills and sources of evidence in carrying out investigations. They present their findings in a coherent way and reach conclusions that are consistent with the evidence.

Task 1

Some students may need help in selecting characters for their broadcast. Possible characters could include:

For tourism:
- Any of the governments who are present in Antarctica
- Airline companies
- Boat companies
- Tour operators
- International Association of Antarctican Tour Operators
- A tourist who would like to visit Antarctica
- City officials from port towns.

Against tourism:
- Any of the governments present in Antarctica
- Greenpeace
- Australian Conservation Foundation
- Wilderness Society
- Any other NGO that the student may be familiar with who could have a role in the Antarctic.

Level 3

Just description/listing of the advantages and disadvantages from the photos, which are randomly given to different characters.
- Character one: 'I am against tourism because 6000 king penguins were killed in a stampede when visitors came to view them.'
- Character 2: 'I am for tourism because it could give money for government scientific operations and justify claims to Antarctic territory.'

Level 4

Mainly descriptions and listings of advantages and disadvantages from the photos which are given to characters but put into a logical order for example:
- Character one: 'The damage by tourism may be less than that compared with the construction and refuse of Antarctic bases.'
- Character two: 'There will be increased demands for free land and fresh water supply, disposal of sewage and rubbish.'

Level 5

The student not only uses the photos as a source of contrasting view but also uses the remaining text to strengthen the argument and develop good explanations. The student backs the radio broadcast up with statistics. For example:
- Character one: 'Only 4 per cent of Antarctica is not covered by ice, we cannot afford to have tourism on such a small area of land when the damage from a footprint in the moss may last for 10 years.'
- Character two: 'Tourism can be managed carefully. I would recommend using overflights, but not at a low height as I don't want to cause disturbance to the wildlife. We will of course need more search and rescue backup to avoid the problems highlighted by the Mount Erebus disaster of 1979.'

There is a conclusion to the broadcast based on the evidence presented. The student may have selected extra information from the Internet or other reference sources.

Level 6

The student uses all the source materials and constructs a very interesting debate between the characters. Statistics are used. The student also draws on information and terminology from the previous units and uses words such as 'ecotourism' and 'sustainable'. For example:

- Character one: 'If ecotourism is recommended in Antarctica we must ensure that we stick to its principles and don't destroy the very resource that people have come to look at. Tourism must be sustainable. We cannot allow over 6000 people to visit Antarctica and all tread on moss and leave footprints which will not disappear for 10 years.'
- Character two: 'The slow colonisation of plants and the slow formation of soil mean that tourism can never be truly sustainable in Antarctica. If people are true eco-

tourists, they will know about the Antarctic ecology and will not want to risk damaging it. Setting foot in one of the planes is not showing respect for the environment. Planes use up a tremendous amount of fuel.'

The conclusion to the broadcast relates to the evidence presented in the debate. The student will have used sources of information from the Internet or other reference sources.

Alternative assessment methods

This assessment lends itself to:

- oral assessment. The script could be acted out instead of written at length. The work could be recorded onto tape.
- group assessment. Groups of four/five students could plan the broadcast. Each person would be assessed on their particular speech.

POPULATION

The global family

The global family officially stood at six billion strong on 12 October 1999; according to the United Nations.

This is just two months after the population of India officially passed the one billion mark, although in terms of pure numbers China still out strips its neighbour; it is thought that within little more than a decade India, which has twice the birth rate of China, will take over as the most populous country on Earth.

To give an idea of quite how fast we humans are spawning, the UN first marked World Population Day in 1987 to celebrate the passing of 5 billion.

'Reaching six billion marks a success,' said UN Population fund's Executive Director, Dr Nafis Sadik. 'People are living longer and healthier lives than any other generation in history. But it is also a challenge,' she said.

'Today there are over a billion young people between 15 and 24 years of age. Their decisions about the size and spacing of their families will determine how many people will be on the planet by 2050 and beyond. Their decisions will also help to determine how they live – in poverty or prosperity; on a green and healthy planet or in a world devastated by human activities.'

'Good outcomes depend on good choices,' Dr Sadik continued. 'And good choices depend on freedom to choose, for women and men alike, in all areas of life.'

Every year the world population grows by about 78 million people. It took all of time for population to reach the one billion level in 1804. However it took just 123 years to reach the two billion in 1927, and only 33 years more to reach three billion in 1960. Fourteen years later in 1974, it reached four billion.

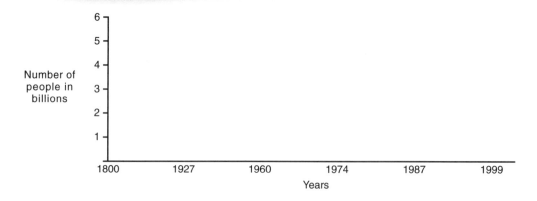

QUESTIONS

1 Using the figures quoted in the above passage, complete the graph to show world population growth.

2 What do you notice about the speed of growth of world population?

3 What could affect the growth in the future?

4 Why do you think that India will overtake China as the world's most populated country?

Girl power in India

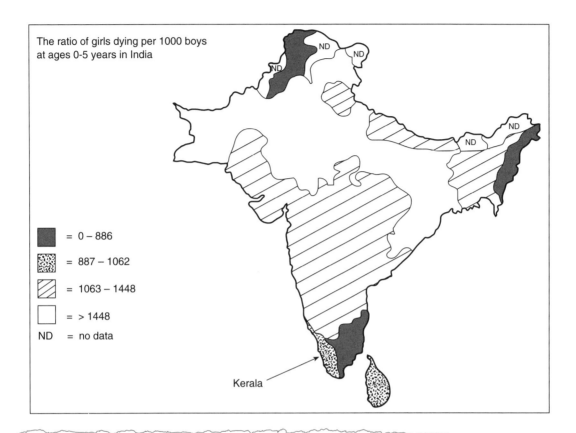

The ratio of girls dying per 1000 boys at ages 0-5 years in India

■ = 0 – 886

▨ = 887 – 1062

▧ = 1063 – 1448

☐ = > 1448

ND = no data

Kerala

In Sreekariyam, in the southern Indian state of Kerala, childless couple Josy and Nera have spent more than a year awaiting news from a local adoption centre. Since their application was approved, the agency has three times offered them a baby boy – yet the couple have decided to hold out for their first choice.

'Both of us have agreed that we will wait for a girl,' the future father says. Their determination is not unusual in Kerala: recent statistics from the state's main adoption centre reveal that Keralites prefer girls.

A few thousand kilometres away in the Indian capital of New Delhi, the attitudes of adopting couples couldn't be more different.

'If we adopt a girl she will have to be married off with a huge dowry,' says Shivagi, a prospective parent who expects a boy to support her in her old age. 'We can't afford a girl.'

Killing girl babies still happens in both India and China.

In India nearly 300,000 more girls than boys die annually in childhood because they are neglected when ill and not given enough food. Although banned in many states, sex selection testing has been widely available, leading to aborting of female foetuses. 25 per cent of the 12 million baby girls who are born in India each year do not survive to be 15 because of the low value society gives them.

In Kerala the situation is different. Here women have equal rights, they inherit land, and they are nearly all literate, which means that they have helped to change the idea that only men can be breadwinners and support elderly parents. In the northern state of Punjab only sons can inherit land.

 'Girl Power', *Developments Magazine* 1999

QUESTIONS

1 What is the difference between the number of girls and boys dying in the north and south of India?

2 What reason is given for there being more boys than girls born in India?

3 Why is Kerala one of the few states where there are more girls than boys?

Quality of life in cities

CITY	MURDERS PER 100,000	FOOD COSTS % INCOME	LIVING SPACE PEOPLE PER ROOM	% HOMES WITH WATER AND ELECTRICITY	% TELEPHONES	% 14–17 YEAR OLDS IN SECONDARY SCHOOL	INFANT MORTALITY PER 1000	PEACE AND QUIET 1=NOISY, 10=QUIET	TRAFFIC FLOW MPH IN RUSH HOUR	URBAN LIVING STANDARDS SCORE
Dhaka	2.4	63	3.1	73	2	37	108	4	21.4	32
Singapore	2.0	38	1.2	100	46	82	7	2	37.3	79
Birmingham	1.8	20	0.5	100	50	66	11	7	2	77
London	2.5	24	0.6	100	50	58	10	3	10.4	69
Manchester	0.9	34	0.7	100	64	76	10	9	4	81

Urban living standards: 75+ very good, 60 good, 45 fair, below 45 poor.

QUESTIONS

1 How do the overall quality of life scores in Dhaka and Singapore vary?

2 Which thing is better in Dhaka than in Singapore?

3 What do you think causes these differences in quality of life?

4 Compare the British cities with Singapore. Although the scores are similar, pick out the things that are different about the quality of life in Singapore, Birmingham, London and Manchester.

5 What things would you have to improve to increase the quality of life index in Birmingham, London and Manchester?

Not so old in Oldham

THE BEST AREAS FOR A LONG LIFE

Where you live in Britain has become an increasing factor in your chances of dying prematurely, a report showed today.

The survey has highlighted a widening North–South divide, with residents in Oldham, Salford and Greenock having mortality rates almost a third higher than the national average. Dr Dorling examined death rates for infants, adolescents and adults by sex throughout England, Scotland and Wales.

The figures showed that:

- Glasgow residents were 68 per cent more likely to die prematurely than people living in rural Dorset, and 31 per cent more likely than those living in Bristol.
- A baby girl born in Leeds is more than twice as likely to die in the first year of life than an infant growing up in a town in Dorset.
- Death rates for baby boys in Blackburn, Halifax and Preston are almost double the national average.
- Eight times as many boys aged one to four died in Manchester between 1990 and 1992 as died in Gloucestershire.

Dr Dorling said 'These patterns of varying life chances need to be investigated – and that is likely to prove a harder task than describing them.'

As part of the World Health Organisation's Targets for Health, Britain has made a commitment to reduce health inequalities by the year 2000.

QUESTIONS

1 What would you investigate if you were Dr Dorling? Make a list of things which might affect the death rates in different parts of the country.

2 How could you actually investigate these things? Make a list of how you would collect the information.

3 Why can looking at the average life expectancy for a country be misleading?

The shape of the UK

Nearly a quarter of women who are in their late 20s will not have had children by the time they are 45, according to new statistics.

The 1996 figures on births in England and Wales shows that about 23 per cent of women born in 1971 are projected to be childless by the time they are 45, in 2016.

The figures show a major shift in the number of women choosing to have children. Statistics from 1946 predicted that only 9 per cent of women would be childless by middle age.

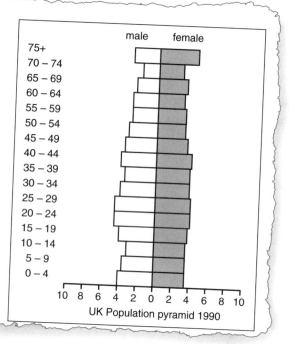

UK Population pyramid 1990

QUESTIONS

1 Describe what this population pyramid shows about the UK's population.

2 Add up the total percentage of elderly people (age 65 upwards) shown on this population pyramid.

3 Add up the total percentage of young people from 0–19.

4 Add the number of people from the working population (20–64).

5 How many working people are there compared to dependants?

6 Use the article above and other information you have already read to help you to draw a sketch of the shape of a population pyramid for the UK in 2031.

7 What do you think will happen to the figures you have calculated in questions 2, 3, 4 and 5?

Commentary on the questions

Student Book

Population (pages 94–95)

High densities may lead to differences in the quality of life. In rich cities such as Singapore city, there will be some environmental problems associated with living in a large city. It is expensive to drive into Singapore city and so the people use the brilliant public transport systems such as an advanced metro. The quality of housing is good on the whole. Singapore has also encouraged people to have smaller families by using incentive systems. In Dacca poverty prevents such revolutionary transport management. The key issue here is the poor quality of the housing. There is a lot of unemployment. Many people have come to Dacca having fled problems such as flooding and poverty in the countryside.

1 Europe and Asia.

2 New York, Los Angeles, Mexico City, Sao Paulo, Buenos Aires, Bombay, Calcutta, Beijing, Shanghai, Tokyo, Seoul.
   a With the exception of Mexico City all are on the coast. Most are in poorer countries.
   b On the coast.
   c New York, Los Angeles, Tokyo, Seoul have a good standard of living. They have more money to overcome the problems of high densities.
   Mexico city, Sao Paulo, Buenos Aires, Bombay, Beijing, Shanghai, Calcutta would have a lower standard of living because they are in poorer countries.

Living on the edge (pages 96–97)

1 Too cold: e.g., Arctic, Antarctic, tops of high mountain ranges.
   Too hot: deserts, rainforests; too wet: swamps and marshes, e.g. Everglades, Florida; too high: high mountain ranges; too steep: high mountain ranges.

2 Desert: little water, too hot in day and cold at night. Tropical forests: humid, difficult access, poor soils when forest cut down; Arctic/Antarctic: too cold, dark for half of the year, nothing grows; Swamps: cannot grow crops, some diseases such as malaria.

3 The environment affects the ability of people to survive. In poorer countries the people are the country's resources so there tends to be more of them. In other countries people are replaced by technology.

Policies from the cradle to the grave (pages 98–99)

1 If students do not know their family, then they could do the Royal family instead.

2 They are more independent and often have jobs. They do not need boys to ensure help in the future. They are also wealthier and provide medicine for their children ensuring their survival.

3 a Africa, Asia and South America.
   b One-child policies which lead to improving lifestyle. Health schemes enhance status of women.

4 a Europe and Asia.
   b They could increase family allowances or offer bonus payments for children and better childcare arrangements for working parents.

5 The higher the GNP the lower the population growth rates.

6 Increase the per capita income and increasing the skills and opportunities for women. Force people to have fewer children as in the case of China.

China's policy for a growing population (pages 100–101)

1 a Most of China's population are on the arable lands of the east coast.

2 a Both birth and death rates were dramatically lowered.

3 a The number of young people under 15 has reduced from 7.8 per cent in 1953 to 4 per cent in 1995.
   b There is a noticeable increase in the number of over 85s.
   c In 1953 there were roughly the same numbers of girls and boys. In 1964 there were 0.2 per cent more boys, by 1982 there were 5 per cent boys and 4. 5 per cent girls. By 1995 there were 4 per cent boys and 3.2 per cent girls.
   d One-child policy has favoured boys and reduced the number of young people. The country has benefited from a reduction in young dependent people and has provided better health care. More elderly people live longer.

4 C = 1960s, F = 1980, G = 1984. Others are more flexible.

The many faces of China (pages 102–103)

1 a/b Boys survive, girls do not.

2 You would be well fed and have a good education. You would have a lot of relatives who depend on you financially and socially later in life.

3 The one-child policy reduced China's population. There is a well educated and well fed workforce and standards of living have increased. There is an imbalance with more boys than girls, plus human rights issues linked to this. The population is ageing and future generations will find difficulties in managing the elderly.

Lifestyles for growth (pages 104–105)

2 a Only 23 per cent of the women are literate.
   b Children are part of the economic and social success of the family.

Britain's going grey (pages 106–107)

1 17 million.

2 28.8 per cent.

3 There may not be enough money to treat them all in the NHS or to pay all the pensions. Fewer young people paying taxes leads to higher taxes or people will be encouraged to make provision for their own pensions.

4 a They depend on others financially and socially.
   b The young are not old enough to look after themselves. The elderly may be infirm.

An agenda for the 21st century (pages 108–109)

2 There are cost savings involved.

Extensions (page 110)

1 a Iceland, Oman and Brazil.
   b Iceland is too cold, Oman is a desert country and Brazil has a lot of inaccessible rainforest.
   c They are wealthy countries. Bahrain can overcome its desert environment because it has a wealthy oil industry. The Netherlands has a wealthy industrial base.

2 b Algeria, natural increase 24.4 per cent.
      Germany – 1 per cent.
      Mozambique – 26 per cent.
      Canada – 6 per cent.
      Italy – 0 per cent.
   c Mozambique and Algeria may want to reduce their population growth rate. Lower the birth rate by encouraging more birth control, increase the literacy rates among women, improve the status of women and encourage them not to depend on their children financially, educate people about the links between environment and population growth. One-child policies or policies which reward people who have fewer children.
   d Germany, Italy and Canada. Offer financial incentives such as extra child benefit. Make it easier for families to work and have children by providing better childcare and by making employers more child friendly.

3 a India and Niger are the poorest and the UK and Germany are the richest
   b True   False   True.
   c Both infant mortality and GNP are directly linked to the fertility rate of countries.
      • Low GNP will affect infant mortality because it will mean poor health care affecting the choice of women so that they have more children.

4 a Kenya has many children under 15 and few people over 65, USA has few children under 15 and many more over 65. The USA has more women over 65 than men.

   b Kenya will need a lot of ante-natal care, vaccinations, post-natal care, schools. USA will have a lot of elderly people to look after. The government will have to provide nursing homes, pensions, more recreational activities for them.
   c In Kenya population control policies, similar to the 4 pillars in India. The USA they will need to encourage people to plan for retirement to prevent health problems, to invest for pensions. They will need to make sure there are enough facilities for people such as nursing homes. There will be fewer younger relatives to support them.

Homework and Assessment Book
Worksheet 31: Girl power in India (page 59)

1 Many more girls die in the north than do in the south.

2 People want boys because they are traditionally the main breadwinners and the girls have expensive dowries.

3 Women are equal in Kerala which means that they do not have to rely on a son for their future.

Worksheet 32: Quality of life in cities (page 60)

1 Dhaka has low and Singapore has high quality rating.

2 Dhaka is quieter.

3 Money probably causes all of these differences.

4 Traffic is worse in the UK but Singapore has less living space. Singapore has better education, lower infant mortality but is also noisier.

5 You would need to improve traffic, reduce murders in London and increase education.

Worksheet 33: Not so old in Oldham (page 61)

1 Smoking figures, health spending, infant mortality.

2 Census data, surveys, market research, performance figures, state of the environment reports.

3 Areas have different averages.

Worksheet 34: The shape of the UK (page 62)

1 It is an ageing population with two sets of boom years 25–29 and 44–49 (1990 data).

2 175.   3 26 per cent.   4 58 per cent.

5 58 per cent working and 42 per cent dependant.

7 Narrower base and more elderly at the top.